CONTENTS

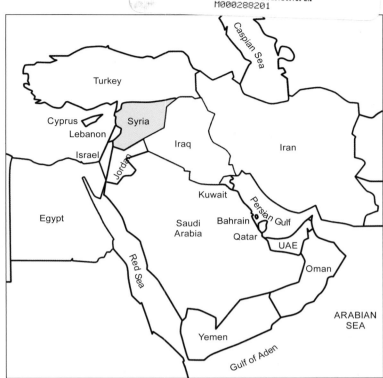

Helion & Company Limited
Unit 8 Amherst Business Centre
Budbrooke Road
Warwick
CV34 5WE
England
Tel. 01926 499 619
Fax 0121 711 4075
Email: info@helion.co.uk
Website: www.helion.co.uk
Twitter: @helionbooks
Visit our blog http://blog.helion.co.uk/

Published by Helion & Company 2018
Designed and typeset by Mach 3 Solutions Ltd (www.mach3solutions.co.uk)
Cover designed by Paul Hewitt, Battlefield Design (www.battlefield-design.co.uk)
Printed by Henry Ling Limited, Dorchester, Dorset

Text © Tom Cooper 2018
Images © as individually credited
Colour profiles © Tom Cooper 2018
Maps © Tom Cooper 2018

ISBN 978-1-912390-37-3

British Library Cataloguing-in-Publication Data.
A catalogue record for this book is available from the British Library.

For details of other military history titles published by Helion & Company
Limited contact the above address, or visit our website: http://www.helion.co.uk.

We always welcome receiving book proposals from prospective authors.

Cover Images

Russian Su-34 at Hmeimim AB (main photo) and (artwork): this MiG-23MF (serial number 2657) was one of the last three aircraft of 678 Squadron, SyAAF, as of late 2015 – early 2018. It still wore the insignia of 'The Works' (central maintenance facility of the SyAAF, situated at Nayrab AB, outside Aleppo) on the nose, between the radome and serial. (Artwork by Tom Cooper)

Note

In order to simplify the use of this book, all names, locations and geographic designations are as provided in The Times World Atlas, or other traditionally accepted major sources of reference, as of the time of described events. Similarly, Arabic names are romanised and transcripted rather than transliterated. For example: the definite article al- before words starting with 'sun letters' is given as pronounced instead of simply as al- (which is the usual practice for non-Arabic speakers in most English-language literature and media).

Introduction and Acknowledgments

Mid-way through September 2015, reports began to surface – first from sources in the country, then in the social media, and finally in the mainstream media (MSN) – about the appearance of Russian-speaking troops and of combat vehicles only operated by the Russian Army, then about the arrival of aircraft of the Russian Air-Space Force (Vozdushno-Kosmicheskiye Sily, VKS) in Syria, and then about their involvement in combat operations. Hard to believe early on, rumours quickly turned into reality, and it became clear: the Russian Federation had launched a military intervention in Syria on behalf of the government of Bashar al-Assad, notorious for systematic killing of its oppositionals, on an industrial scale, for decades, and the frequent deployment of chemical weapons. Despite repeated announcements about a 'withdrawal' of its forces from Syria, the same military intervention is still going on at the time of writing: indeed, the war in Syria is still very much being fought as the work on this narrative was concluded, and this is likely to remain that way for a number of years longer.

Amid a flurry of related reporting, discerning the hard facts from a massive propaganda campaign launched by Moscow, and diverse other 'ambient noise', has proven exceptionally hard. Indeed, the prevalent public impression about the nature and flow of the Syrian War often borders on science fiction. While this is unsurprising considering the amount of factually wrong, and often intentionally misleading, reporting by many diverse sources over the years, and incredible amounts of fateful, yet wrong decisions by the decision-makers involved, the tragic fact is that this conflict meanwhile rarely catches the attention of the MSN. Indeed, after seven years of this war, there is less in-depth reporting than ever before, and 'purely' military-related studies remain as scarce as snake's sweat.

The principal question related to this project was thus always the one of obtaining enough reliable and enough supportable information necessary for a sober analysis, i.e. the question of methodology. In my work, I see my duty foremost as that of a moderator: somebody introducing the reader to the topic through presenting the historic, geographic, and socio-political backgrounds for the conflict in question, and then presenting data and recollections of participants, preferably collected in the course of personal interviews. Therefore, I am always on the search for contacts to participants, and try as hard as possible – and as safely for my sources as possible – to obtain information from them. After all, there is no doubt that the participants are – consciously or not – in possession of the knowledge about what is going on ('on the ground', but in the air, too); which armed groups are around and about their capabilities and intentions; what weapons systems are being used, and what are the 'lessons learned'. My experiences have taught me to appreciate second- and third-hand sources: while knowledge of local people, their culture, traditions, habits, and sourcing information from first-hand sources are of paramount importance for quality of information and resulting analysis, participants rarely have the so-called 'big picture'. On the contrary, their insights can often be enriched by questions, observations, conclusions, even critique from 'outsiders'.

Therefore, and as usual, this book came into being on the basis of extensive interviews with numerous first-hand sources – rather few participants, but plenty of what can be described as 'eyewitnesses'. The information they have provided was then cross-examined with a myriad of second- and third-hand sources. I would never claim that I have got everything 'right', even less so that I have got anything like 'the only truth': despite all the best efforts of everybody involved, this book is likely to contain a mass of mistakes. In the case of ongoing conflicts, I find this more than 'natural': far too many exact details about specific armed groups involved in the war in Syria remain unclear, and are likely to remain that way for a while longer – and that is without talking about the reasons for specific steps taken by crucial decision-makers, or the precise planning and flow of combat operations. Moreover, I am perfectly aware of the fact that conflict analysis is never a 'neutral activity'. Regardless of circumstances under which it is run, and regardless of by whom, it is – de-facto – an 'intervention' in itself: the analysis of the sources alone is often a hotly disputed issue between serious observers, not to mention the methods of data collection, or related conclusions. Furthermore, the background and personal preferences of every analyst performing data collection and analysis are 100 percent certain to have a direct impact upon the reliability and credibility of the result. Therefore, the result – or at least various of its parts – of my work in this case is likely to surprise some, anger others, even prompt disparaging reactions by many, and then also appear as 'nothing new' for quite a few observers. Nevertheless, I do hope that 'Moscow's Game of Poker' – large parts of which originally came into being as articles prepared for the magazine Truppendienst, published by the Austrian Ministry of Defence, but also as short pieces for other specialised defence-related publications around the globe – might help understand not only in what fashion and under what circumstances the military of the Russian Federation became embroiled in as dirty and bloody a civil war as that in Syria, but also about what exactly is it has been doing there since 2015. Foremost, I hope it might contribute to a better understanding of the Russian Federation's military capabilities and intentions in general, and be of some use for further initiatives in this direction: after all, conflict analysis is not a one-time task; it run in serious fashion – it never ends.

There is little doubt that much of my research for this book is based on my travels to Syria in the 2000s. While resulting in the establishment of relatively few direct links to principal protagonists of the combat operations described in this book, the trips in question did help me get in touch with a number of well-positioned military officers in that country. Like everywhere else around the globe, those amongst them that are still in active service are strictly prohibited from having any kind of contacts to foreigners: related interviews have always had to be run clandestinely, and there is no way I could publicly express my gratitude for all the help I have received from them. The reader might want to keep in mind that the names of sources in Syria would hardly mean anything to anybody outside specific circles inside that country's military, and is advised that all the information sourced from such contacts was obtained at immense risk for the people providing it: that the government and security services loyal to Bashar al-Assad are running an outright campaign of 'disappearing' – or at least 'punishing' – even family members of anybody showing the slightest trace of disloyalty. For this reason, I have to express my gratitude in private to all those who are still serving, have either retired from their service or have meanwhile left Syria, and have supported my work over time.

Of others who have helped in this project, I would like to forward my special thanks to Milos Sipos, from Slovakia: thanks to his patient collection of thousands of related news reports on the ACIG.info forum over the years, it proved far easier to monitor this conflict, but also to collect third-hand sources of reference. For similar reasons, I would like to express my special thanks to Aaron Morris in the USA. Furthermore, Tomislav Mesaric, former pilot of the Croatian Air Force, has helped immensely with his studies of modern Russian military equipment. Last, but not least, I can never express enough gratitude to my dear wife, whose patience, understanding, but also help with further research have significantly contributed to the realisation of this project.

Glossary and abbreviations

AAM	air-to-air missile
AB	air base
An	Antonov (the design bureau led by Oleg Antonov)
AI	Amnesty International
ASCC	Air Standardisation Coordinating Committee
AQI	al-Qaeda in Iraq (jihadist movement with Wahhabist ideology, which split from original al-Qaeda)
ATMS	automated tactical management system
AWACS	airborne early warning and control system
BVR	beyond visual range
CBU	cluster bomb unit
CENTCOM	Central Command (of the US military)
CO	commanding officer
COIN	counter-insurgency
COMINT	communications intelligence
ECM	electronic countermeasures
ECCM	electronic counter-countermeasures
ELINT	electronic intelligence
FAC	forward air controller
FSyA	Free Syrian Army
GenStab	Russian General Staff (equivalent to the Joint Chiefs of Staff)
GLONASS	globalnaya navigatsionnaya sputnikovaya systema (global navigation satellite system)
GRF	Group of Russian Federation's Forces in Syria
HQ	headquarters
HRW	Human Rights Watch
HUD	head-up display
HTS	Harakat Tahrir ash-Sham (re-designation of the JAN in 2017)
IADS	integrated air defence system
IAI	Israeli Aircraft Industries
IAP	international airport
IASF	Israeli Air-Space Force (since 2004)
IDF	Israeli Defence Force
IDF/AF	Israeli Defence Force/Air Force (until 2004)
IDP	internally displaced person
IED	improvised explosive device
IFV	infantry fighting vehicle
IHL	International Humanitarian Law
Il	Ilyushin (the design bureau led by Sergey Vladimirovich Ilyushin, also known as OKB-39)
IRGC	Islamic Revolutionary Guards Corps (also 'Sepah')
IRIAF	Islamic Republic of Iran Air Force
IS	Islamic State (colloquially 'Daesh')
JAF	Jaysh al-Fateh (coalition of diverse Syrian insurgent movements and the JAN active in Idlib of 2015 and 2016)
JAN	Jabhat an-Nusra (jihadist movement with Wahhabist ideology, linked to al-Qaeda)
JFS	Jabhat Fateh ash-Sham (re-designation of the JAN in 2016)
MANPAD	man-portable air defence (system)
MiG	Mikoyan i Gurevich (the design bureau led by Artyom Ivanovich Mikoyan and Mikhail Iosifovich Gurevich, also known as OKB-155 or MMZ 'Zenit')
MOD	Ministry of Defence
MSF	Médicins Sans Frontiers
NATO	North Atlantic Treaty Organisation
nav/attack	navigational and attack (avionics suite)
OKB	Opytno-Konstrooktorskoye Byuro (design bureau)
PMC	private military company
RF	Russian Federation
RGD	Republican Guards Division
RHAW	radar homing and warning (system)
RTP	Rastan-Talbiseh Pocket (insurgent-controlled area north of Homs)
RWR	radar warning receiver
SAA	Syrian Arab Army
SAM	surface-to-air missile
SAR	search and rescue
SARC	Syrian Association of Red Crescent
SDF	Syrian Democratic Forces (US proxy dominated by the Kurdish PKK/PYD/YPG/YPJ-conglomerate)
SIGINT	signals intelligence
STOL	short takeoff and landing
Sqn	squadron
Su	Sukhoi (the design bureau led by Pavel Ossipovich Sukhoi, also known as OKB-51)
SVBIED	suicide vehicle-borne improvised explosive device
SyAAF	Syrian Arab Air Force
SyAADF	Syrian Arab Air Defence Force
THK	Türk Havva Kuvvetleri (Turkish Air Force)
TLAM	Tomahawk Land Attack Missile (also BGM-109)
UN	United Nations
USAF	United States Air Force
USN	US Navy
USSR	Union of Soviet Socialist Republics (also 'Soviet Union')
VG	variable geometry (wing)
VKS	Vozdushno-Kosmicheskiye Sily (Russian Air-Space Force)
WHO	World Health Organisation

CHAPTER 1
GEO-STRATEGIC BACKGROUNDS

With 15 March 2018, the civil war in Syria has entered its seventh year. This extremely brutal and bloody conflict has long been far more than 'just' a 'civil war': it is a war with geostrategic dimensions, the effects of which can be felt all over the World.

Curiously, this conflict began quite small: following public protesting in Dera'a and Damascus, in February 2011, during which the participants demanded an end to the corrupt economic policies. The protest movement – which involved all ethnic and religious groups, and all segments of Syrian society – widened to Homs and Hama, then to Aleppo. While announcing 'comprehensive reforms', the government of President Bashar al-Assad showed no sympathy, and even less understanding or readiness to compromise. Blaming 'radical Salafists' and a 'foreign conspiracy', it deployed various of its security services and 'elite' units of its regular military, and then activated diverse criminal gangs to crush the protesting in blood. These conducted not only armed attacks on protesters, but also extensive raids, mass arrests, arbitrary detention, torture and the systematic killing of dozens of thousands of oppositionals. In particular, the activities of such elements against the demonstrators in Dera'a, in the period between 14 and 27 March 2011 – in the course of which even school children were murdered under torture – caused widespread outrage throughout the country. These actions resulted in mass desertions of the military, and a few of regular units of the Syrian Arab Army (SAA) even turned their arms against each other. Through May and June 2011, the deserters began organizing themselves into armed groups, which subsequently began to refer to themselves as the Free Syrian Army (FSyA). Although largely unreported outside Syria, desertions reached such proportions that the military shrank to less than one-third of its pre-war strength by the end of 2011, and was forced to disband nearly two thirds of its brigades and its entire air defence branch. The Assad government then de-facto dissolved the remaining units by distributing these to about 2000 different check-points around the country, making any kind of effective control over them impossible. For all practical purposes, and with the exception of the air force, the regular military of Syria ceased to exist by the end of 2012.[1]

Tragically, the insurgency failed to exploit the momentum: while bringing most of Aleppo (city) and large parts of south-western Syria under its control, it suffered extensive losses in Damascus and Hama, and found itself besieged in northern Homs. Moreover, although up to 7,000 diverse armed groups came into being through 2012, the leadership of the FSyA never managed to establish a uniform structure and a centralized organisation. Primarily due to immense pressure from outside powers – initially Turkey and the USA, later Qatar, Kuwait, Saudi Arabia and the United Arab Emirates, all of which demanded concessions and formal declarations regarding their ideological and religious orientation in exchange for assistance – deep rifts emerged within the ranks of the armed opposition. These were exploited by foreign powers to – in exchange for money, food, and arms – literally buy concessions from selected major insurgent groups. Furthermore, the government in Damascus went to extremes to tarnish the reputation of the insurgency, and seed disunity within. While detaining and then disappearing dozens of thousands of entirely peaceful activists and oppositionals, it freed thousands of Islamists from its prisons. With some help from Damascus, and even more so from abroad, many of the latter were to play the crucial role in the emergence of armed groups of so-called 'Salafi jihadists' – actually followers of militant Wahhabism with ties to the al-Qaeda. Finally, the various security services of Damascus launched a campaign of massacres of selected ethnic groups, with the aim of causing an inter-ethnic and inter-religious strife, and separating the Sunni majority from members of the opposition with other different ethnic and religious backgrounds.[2]

Unsurprisingly for a country as impoverished as Syria, and especially in a protracted war, supplies – whether in the form of money, combatants, arms or other means – are essential. By mid-2012, the insurgency was split into multiple groups with religiously motivated-factions growing in size and influence. Indeed, enjoying ever growing support from abroad, extremist groups – foremost the notorious Jabhat an-Nusra (JAN), composed of up to 70 percent transnational jihadists, and linked directly to al-Qaeda – proved capable of not only attracting additional fighters through the provision of regular salaries, arms, ammunition and food, but also through social commitment. On the contrary, Western powers in particular have limited their aid to a handful of hand-picked groups that began losing influence, and then primarily in the form of the provision of so-called non-lethal aid, including limited amounts of communication equipment and some training. In the long term, this led to widespread disappointment and distancing of the Syrian insurgency and the West.

The year 2012 also saw the onset of the military intervention by the Islamic Republic of Iran – a longstanding ally of the Assad government. Tehran reacted cautiously to the protesting and then a popular uprising in the country, early on, and deployed only several limited contingents of 'advisors' from the Islamic Revolutionary Guards Corps (IRGC, also 'Army of the Guardians of the Islamic Revolution'). However, as the desertions of the Syrian military personnel began reaching dramatic proportions, the influence and importance of the IRGC's involvement continued to grow – in numbers and importance. In late 2012, Tehran had ordered the Hezbollah ('Party of God') – a Shi'a Islamist militia from Lebanon that it created in the 1980s – into a military intervention in Syria, and in early 2013 began deploying its own units in the Syrian capital. Over the following years, the IRGC began literally flooding Syria with ever more para-military formations of its proxies: whether from Iran, Iraq, Afghanistan, Pakistan, or even Azerbaijan, most of these prided themselves as belonging to the 'Axis of Islamic Resistance', and could only be described as 'Shi'a jihadists'.

Despite countless denials from Damascus and Tehran, and even more so from their supporters at home and abroad, the IRGC has not only maintained a permanent military presence in Syria ever since: it is playing the role that is crucial for the very survival of the Assad government. The reasons for such involvement are not limited to the military situation or provision of far more arms, ammunition and combatants than the West and all of its allies have provided to the opposition, combined: but because the Assad government bankrupted itself on the financial level, Tehran is helping it to survive through generous funding.[3] Moreover, the Iranians began seeking to integrate themselves within the Shi'a minority of Syria, while simultaneously recruiting and funding the creation of dozens of diverse militias from Syria and Iraq, pan-Arabist militias from Lebanon and Egypt, and a large militia staffed by the second and third generation of Palestinian refugees in Syria. While all are nominally loyal to the Assad government, they are foremost responsible to and commanded by the IRGC. In this fashion, the Iranians have created a para-state that is controlling large portions of the real estate and much of the economy within what are nominally 'government controlled' parts of the country.

On the military level, the interventions of the IRGC and then the Hezbollah resulted in the recovery of most of Homs (city), by the summer of 2013, while the siege of the garrison in government-controlled Western Aleppo was lifted in the autumn of the same year. However, these operations had only temporary effects: much of Damascene suburbs, most of northern and south-western Syria, and half of Aleppo City remained under the control of insurgents. The involvement of the IRGC and Hezbollah thus brought no significant change in the overall flow of the war.

What proved to be the actual point of 'turn-over' in this war was the emergence of the terrorist organisation with an even more extremist ideology than that of al-Qaeda, known as the 'Islamic State' (IS, colloquially 'Daesh'). Founded by officers from the former security apparatus of the government of Saddam Hussein at-Tikriti of Iraq and extremists of the al-Qaeda in Iraq (AQI), the Daesh entered north-eastern Syria with the help of the Assad Government in 2012. Exploiting the Syrian tradition of welcoming the guest, and through a combination of assassinations and subversions, it virtually destroyed the insurgency in north-eastern Syria and, by late 2013, spread to Aleppo, eastern Idlib, Homs, and the eastern outskirts of Damascus. Only a decisive counter-offensive by various native Syrian insurgents – the first ever serious military counterattack on the 'IS' – stopped this advance in early 2014. Nevertheless, and tragically, ever since the sheer presence of the Daesh in Syria has been misused not only by the Assad government, but also by nearly every single foreign power as a pretext against the disunited Syrian insurgency.[4]

While unsuccessful in densely-populated north-western Syria, the Daesh rapidly established itself in control over much of north-western Iraq, provoking not only a Western but also an Iranian military intervention in that country, starting in August 2014. From that point onwards, the Daesh began playing the major role in the Syrian War, too – at least in the minds of Western decision-makers, and the media in particular: a month later, the USA and most of its Western allies had launched a war against the IS in Syria.

In early 2015, Turkey and Qatar set up a coalition of the JAN and most of the insurgent groups in north-western Syria and helped these wrestle the control of Idlib (city), and deliver crushing blows upon the remnants of the Assad government's military. By the early summer of the same year, the JAN and Syrian insurgents advanced well into the north-eastern Lattakia and northern Hama provinces.

At this point in time, a series of dramatic, theoretically unrelated events took place, which was to exercise strong influence upon the subsequent flow of this war. In July 2015, the United States of America (USA, also US), France, United Kingdom and Germany finalized negotiations for the so-called Joint Comprehensive Plan of Action (JCPOA) Treaty with Iran. Commonly known as the 'Iran nuclear deal', this was a formal regulation along which Tehran agreed to eliminate its stockpiles of medium-enriched uranium, cut its stockpile of low-enriched uranium, dramatically reduced the number of its gas centrifuges, and promised not to build any new heavy-water facilities over a period of 13-15 years. In exchange, the Western powers proposed to gradually lift nuclear-related economic sanctions against the Islamic Republic of Iran – but also to respect Tehran's 'special interests' in Syria. Correspondingly, the West began curbing its support for Syrian insurgents, while exercising pressure upon its local allies to follow in fashion. In March 2015, Saudi Arabia and most of the other members of the Gulf Cooperation Council (GCC) became involved in the protracted, complex and costly war in Yemen. Finally, in the light of growing influence of not only the JAN, but also other conservative Islamist movements within the Syrian insurgency, the USA arrived at the decision to stop supporting the latter. Determined to defeat the 'effects' – i.e. the Daesh – while ignoring the 'cause' – the Assad government – Washington went as far as to demonstratively select a conglomerate dominated by the Kurdish organisation from Turkey, the PKK – listed as a 'terrorist' group in the USA, most of the EU and NATO, and which imposed itself upon the population northern Syria in the form of the PYD party, and its militias, YPG and YPJ – as its new proxy in Syria.[5]

Meanwhile, with the Assad government on the verge of another major defeat, Damascus – perhaps Tehran, too – managed to convince the government of the President of the Russian Federation, Vladimir Putin, that the time was opportune to launch a military intervention in Syria. Already suffering from international isolation and crippling economic embargoes provoked by its invasion of Ukraine a year earlier, and keen to divert public attention at home from the consequences, but also to regain the status of a 'superpower' on the international level, Moscow was more than happy to follow this idea. Abandoning the 30-years old 'tradition' of rather cautious, often reluctant actions of successive governments in Moscow towards the Middle East, but perfectly in the fashion of an entire series of adventures launched since 2008, Putin ordered his military to deploy to Syria in August 2015.

What was to follow was an affair without precedent in Russian history, and one with consequences that are going to be strongly felt in decades to come – not only in Syria or the Middle East, but in all of Europe, the USA, Russia, and even in large parts of Asia.

Syrian Geography

The country that the Russian military found on its arrival in 2015 was dramatically different even to what it was just four years earlier, not to mention the late 1980s – when the last officers of the military of the former Union of Soviet Socialist Republics (USSR, also 'Soviet Union') had left it. The difference began with the way the country looked: while often simply described as a 'desert', and depicted as sand seas or flat rocky deserts in movies, the geography and topography of Syria are extremely diverse. The country stretches for about 830 kilometres (515 miles) on its east-to-west axis, and about 740 kilometres (460 miles) on its north-south axis. In the north-west, Syria has about 193 kilometres (120 miles) of coast on the Mediterranean: this is dominated by a narrow plain extending inland up to around 32 kilometres (20 miles). The coast is separated from the rest of the country by the massive Jebel an-Nusayriyah range of mountains, the highest peaks of which rise up to 2,000 metres (6,561ft) and are often snow-caped well into April and May. The southern end of the Jebel an-Nusayriyah is marked by the so-called Homs Gap – a relatively flat passage and a route that has been used for trade and invaders of all sorts for thousands of years. Further south are the Anti-Lebanon Mountains, peaking with the lofty, 2,814 metre (9,232ft) high Jebel Sheikh (Mount Hermon), before tapering off into a hilly region called the Golan Heights – occupied by Israel since the June 1967 Arab-Israeli War (also known as the 'Six Day War' in the West).

Looking from north towards south, the area east of the mountains starts with the Aleppo Plateau. The fertile terrain there is about 400 metres above sea level, stretching from the valley of the Euphrates in the north-east, to the plains of Idlib in the south-west, the intensively cultivated al-Ghab and Orontes River Valleys in the west, and an arid steppe that forms the northern tip of the Syrian Desert. Also known as the 'Hamad', the latter is about 700 metres above sea level and is not a 'classic sand sea', but a combination of rolling hills – like those of the Palmyra fold belt – and the eastern plateau, all covered by steppe and gravel dotted by shrub grass. Further east and south, the Hamad stretches well into north-eastern Jordan, northern Saudi Arabia, and western Iraq. West of the Hamad, in central Syria, is the so-called 'upland area', including the fertile Homs plateau and the semi-desert of the Qalamoun Range, and also the large and flat Damascus plateau. Supplied with water by the Barada River, sheltered by the Anti-Lebanon Mountains, this area is about 680 metres (2,230ft) above the sea level and dominated by the Ghouta, an irrigated farmland since ancient times.

The climate along the coast is Mediterranean: the area receives plenty of rainfall, is densely populated and intensively cultivated. However, Syria east of the Jebel an-Nusayriyah is characterised by hot, dry summers, and mild, wet winters. Natural vegetation is corresponding: trees and shrubs are plentiful along the coast, there are forests of Aleppo pine and Valonia oak in the Anti-Lebanon Mountains, but the east is dominated by shrubs and reed grasses. While booming in the 19th Century and first decades of the 20th Century, Syria's farmland has subsequently suffered from extensive desertification and soil erosion, caused by the failure of the farmers to practice crop rotation. A combination of irrigation projects launched in the 1960s – partially in reaction to the unilateral Israeli decision to divert the waters of the River Jordan and construction of the National Water Carrier – and improved education of farmers about land management, began showing their effects only during the 1990s, when more of the country – up to 30 percent of its total land area – was made agriculturally productive. Nevertheless, even once about one fifth of the tilled acreage was irrigated, most farmers remained heavily dependent on rainfall to water their crops: indeed, irrigation remained necessary even in most of the regions that continued receiving substantial annual rainfall. Furthermore, due to soil exhaustion, the use of fertilizers is of crucial importance. Unsurprisingly, a combination of drought and overdependence on the government-controlled supply of fertilisers during the late 2000s, have significantly contributed to the unrest that sparked the original civil war in Syria in 2011.

The mountains of Jebel an-Nusayriyah in north-western Syria are covered by dense forests cut by deep canyons. This view is of the Citadel of Salah ed-Din ('Qal'at Salah al-Din', also known as 'Saladin Castle') about 30 kilometres east of Lattakia. (Photo by Tom Cooper)

The landscape of the al-Ghab Plain and the Orontes River Valley is reminiscent of central Europe. (Photo by Tom Cooper)

Typical landscape of the Hamad in the Palmyra area consists of gravel desert dotted with shrub grass. (Photo by Tom Cooper)

Demography of 2015

The population of Syria was, and remains, significantly different to that usually described. During the last census, in 2004, Syria had a population of 17,920,810. Seven years later, this was estimated at 22 million, the majority of whom – about 90 percent – were Arabs, and living in the western parts of the country. Ironically, the usually published break-downs of the country's demographics have stipulated that 65 percent of Syrians are Sunni

Arabs, 12 percent Alawis (an esoteric sect from which most of the governing clique hails), 10 percent Christians, 10 percent Kurds, and three percent Druze (followers of a religion related to Islam). However, the 2004 Census told a dramatically different story: correspondingly, less than nine percent of the Syrians have declared themselves as Alawis, less than five percent as Christians, and less than two percent as the Druze. Although crude, the best guess for the proportion of Kurds was at around 8.5 percent. Indeed, this census has shown that at least 84 percent of Syrians were Sunnis, and at least 75 percent Sunni Arabs.[6]

Furthermore, by the time the Russian military began deploying in the country in summer of 2015, the population of Syria was actually down to just 16.6 million: over 470,000 people were confirmed as killed; another 80,000 as 'disappeared' by the government; over 4 million were registered by the UN as refugees abroad; at least 1 million more were assessed as unregistered, while around 7 million were internally displaced persons (IDPs). Finally, the Assad government was in control of less than 30 percent of the country's territory, and Syria thus ceased to exist as a sovereign country.[7]

In other words: the proportion of the minorities – most of which were wrongly declared as 'supporting the government' – was much smaller than usually claimed; the government was fighting a war against what was certainly the vast majority of the population; and the government was not only short on funding and on troops and had no means to replace losses; but – and unsurprisingly – the war turned more than half of the country's population into homeless refugees, and this primarily because of what was ethnic cleansing of Arab Sunnis. These facts are of particular importance for understanding of exactly what has been going on in Syria since 2011, and especially the behaviour of the Assad government, and its primary foreign supporters.

Shattered Economy

One of the biggest absurdities launched – and insisted upon – by those supporting the government in Damascus regardless what it does, is that Bashar al-Assad is omnipotent and omniscient, but neither related to, nor responsible for any of Syria's problems: on the contrary, all of these have been created by a 'joint conspiracy' of the CIA (i.e. the USA), Mossad (i.e. Israel), and al-Qaeda (often mis-declared as being a 'creation of the USA and Israel, in cooperation with Saudi Arabia'). Actually, the root problem of Syria – the one that caused the war – was, and remains today, an economy shattered by failed policies of the Assad government over the last 40 and more years. This was, and remains, a reflection of what that government did on the political and the military level: a denial of the true dimensions and ramifications of the crisis, avoidance of reality in general, and 'reliance on alternatives'.

In tatters since mid-1970s, and despite periodic improvement, the Syrian economy was severely weakened by the influx of up to three million refugees from Iraq since 2003; the war between Israel and the Hezbollah para-state of the Shi'a Islamist political party and militant group in Lebanon in 2006; drought of the late 2000s; and massive mismanagement of the country's resources by Assad and his closest aides, before, during and after these events. What was originally the Syrian Civil War was thus no accident, nothing that was unavoidable, but a consequence of government failures. As usual, for the first year of the unrest and war, the Assad

government flatly denied the true dimensions and ramifications of the problems it had caused. When facing bankruptcy, and in an attempt to show off its monetary strength, in June 2012 it sold its remaining reserves of hard currencies and gold on the black market. This measure failed to improve the situation: on the contrary, Damascus was forced to request help from Tehran well before that point. Imports of billions of freshly-printed Syrian Lira from Russia only worsened the situation: combined with the lack of stabile sources of income, this resulted in a hyper-inflation and a dramatic decrease of the effective annual budget – from US$16.4 billion in 2010, to 5.1 billion in 2017, as described in Table 1. As mentioned above, Iran jumped in and saved the Assad government through generous funding, most of which was provided clandestinely, in unofficial ways. Tehran provided US$9 billion already by February 2012, followed by another US$6 billion by December 2013 – and in addition to inking the first credit for the supply of crude oil and gas. Similar deals have followed every year ever since. According to the UN, by 2015 Tehran was providing at least US$6 billion, perhaps as much as US$15 billion to Damascus every single year: according to sources in Syria, about a quarter of this aid was delivered in the form of cash, more than a third in the form of crude oil, and the rest in the form of troops paid by the IRGC, and arms, ammunition and food.[8]

Table 1: National Annual Budget of Syria, Real Value, 2010-2017

Year	Value in Syrian Pounds	Value in US$
2010	750 billion	16.4 billion
2011	835 billion	18.3 billion
2012	1326 billion	24.1 billion
2013	1383 billion	20.4 billion
2014	1390 billion	9.9 billion
2015	1554 billion	15.36 billion
2016	1980 billion	7.9 billion
2017	2660 billion	5.1 billion

Sectarian Frenzies

Bashar al-Assad's mismanagement of Syria was not limited to the economy: indeed, its most severe impacts were felt within the military. Because of the Syrian demography, the majority of the Syrian armed forces used to consist of Sunni Arab conscripts. Since the 1960s, a constantly increasing portion of their officers were Alawis, usually appointed for their loyalty to the Assad clan, instead of by merit. The situation worsened after the failed coup attempt of February 1982 (plotted to take place simultaneously with an uprising in Hama): not only were most Sunni officers purged within the following months, but ever since that time, the Assad government and its security services did their utmost to staff the officer corps with members of diverse minorities. Nevertheless, the wave of brutal repression in 2011 still caused multiple waves of defections, and an armed insurrection, not only of Sunni Arabs, but of many Alawis and other ethnic and religious minorities, too.

While the protesting remained entirely peaceful, and the armed uprising spread only slowly for the first six months of the crisis, Damascus then worsened the situation by unleashing a series of sectarian massacres. Once again, this dramatically increased the rate of desertions: by early 2012, more than half of the Syrian military personnel had melted away. Unimpressed, the Assad government continued insisting on declaring the resulting uprising as a 'conspiracy from abroad', 'al-Qaeda related' and 'Islamist terrorism'. This cynical argumentation was used to explain the detention, torture and disappearance of over 80,000 entirely peaceful and secular activists, primarily Sunnis – while at the same time 6,000 extremists were let free from jails, and then supported by the government's security services while recruiting and establishing their own armed militias. Tragically, the result was outright absurd: ignoring open bragging about insane bestialities by the government and its agencies, much of the public and many political decision-makers abroad have accepted this version as 'genuine', and have de-facto declared the Assad government to be the 'lesser of two evils'.[9]

Ironically, because the officers and other ranks that defected early on were some of the most-skilled Syrian military personnel, while the loyalist forces were poorly commanded, the latter suffered extensive losses. By June 2012, up to 50,000 members of loyalist forces were killed or injured in combat. What was left of the SAA – which once used to boast the strength of 20 divisions and about a dozen independent brigades – was about 20 brigade-sized 'task forces': each of these were based on the loyal cadre from one of the former divisions, 'corseted' by detachments from one of the security services and another from the 4th Armoured Division. Even then, the majority of such formations had virtually disintegrated by the end of 2012 – and this on orders from Damascus: because the Assad government defined itself by the levels of control it exercised over the Syrian population, they were broken down to secure about 2,000 checkpoints around the country. With there being no functioning state and no operational military chain of command, there was nobody in position to exercise an effective control over the resulting chaos: the SAA thus ceased to exist as a coherent military force.[10]

'Assad or we burn the country' – graffiti on a wall left behind by 'security' services of the Assad government. (Syrian social media)

Iranians to the Rescue

Unsurprisingly, it was at exactly the same point in time, that Iran launched its own military intervention in Syria. The key conduit for the related decisions was Maher al-Assad, Bashar's younger brother. One of less than a handful of people in Syria in a position to openly express his disagreement with Bashar, Maher was an independent actor with his own financial support, based on a long history of money laundering and the control of multiple business networks. Often at odds with the third major factor in Syria under the Assads, and the third member of the so-called 'Inner Circle' – the Makhlouf clan, Assad's maternal cousins – sometimes with

Bashar too, as a nominal commander of the 4th Armoured Division (the unit is actually commanded by Major-General Mohammad Ali Durgham), and in contact with the IRGC since the 2000s, he was in a position to not only negotiate an Iranian intervention, but also strongly influence the establishment of diverse militias. Indeed, many of these were recruited through Maher's Hossn Association, and have ever since operated as elements of the 4th Armoured Division.[11]

The Iranian military operations in Syria are run by the Qods Corps of the IRGC (also 'Qods Force', IRGC-QF). The IRGC is a separate, para-military branch of the Iranian military, though also one that operates its own ground forces, an air-space force (operating aircraft, helicopters, ballistic missiles, and air defences), and its own navy. Contrary to the regular Iranian military, the IRGC is also a major economic factor, involved eyebrows-deep in all sorts of economic malversations, and meanwhile controlling all major segments of the Iranian economy, including the banking and insurance sectors, telecommunications, transportation, real estate, construction and defence sectors of Iran. Nominally, the IRGC-QF is a branch responsible for para-military operations abroad: in reality, via Vahid Haghanian, it has its own, direct link to what is officially the 'Supreme Leader of the Islamic Revolution', Grand Ayatollah Sayyid Ali Khamenei. Correspondingly, the IRGC-QF acts on direct orders from the head of state and highest ranking political authority in Tehran, and thus enjoys widespread autonomy with regards to its planning, funding, and operations.[12]

The IRGC-QF has maintained ties to the Assad government since the early 1980s, when Damascus began supporting Tehran during the Iran-Iraq War, while Tehran launched the build-up of the Hezbollah in Lebanon as a counter to the Israeli occupation of that country. Over time, the Assad government developed into the closest Iranian ally, prompting numerous officials in Iran to publicly declare the survival of Bashar al-Assad as their 'Red Line'.[13] Having barely survived widespread protesting and a near-uprising over forged election results at home in 2009, Tehran was ill-positioned to publicly announce the launching of a military intervention in Syria. Therefore, after their first two units deployed in Syria suffered extensive losses, the officers of the IRGC-QF were forced to find other solutions.[14] For the purpose of establishing new forces that would fight 'for Assad', they reached back upon legal and para-legal structures that used to exist in Syria from earlier times.[15] The crucial figure in the related operations of the IRGC-QF became its commander, Major-General Qassem Soleimani – officially declared 'the second most important man in Syria' (after Bashar), by the Assad government – and Major-General Hossein Hamedani.[16] The latter – a former commander of the Basiji Corps IRGC, and in 2014 appointed the commander of the IRGC-QF in Syria – recalled the situation on his arrival in 2012 as follows:

> At the start of the conflict the Syrian system did not respond well to peaceful protests and this caused the problem to multiply several times. This response did not come from Bashar Assad's hands. The Baath party has a principle that no one, not even Bashar Assad, can change them. This is why there has not been a coup. An election [in Syria; author's note] is unlike any other: in elections everyone must be a member

of the Baath party. Anyone who wants to be a candidate must have gone through several stages in the party. A person doesn't grow in the party overnight… Therefore, part of the Baath party security has a security problem…the Baath was strong but they didn't create a security force like our country… Only the army was trained to fight wars with the enemy…[17]

The 'popular force' Hamedani described was initially based on gangs of so-called 'Shabiha' ('Ghosts') and consisted of three major, mafia-like, criminal networks originally run by nobody other than members of the extended Assad family. While renowned for their insubordination, these sided with the government early on, were subjected to the control of two top security services, and then converted into private armies on advice from, with help of funding from, and under the control of, the IRGC-QF. In order to secure at least a nominal control over the emerging militias, in 2013 the Air Force Intelligence created the so-called 'Air Force Shield', the centrepiece of which became the 'Tiger Force' ('Quwwat Nimr'): initially an about 1,400-strong formation consisting of about a dozen small, company-sized outfits (20-50 combatants each). In similar fashion, the 'Military Intelligence Branch' ('Su'abat al-Mukhabarat al-Askariya') had established several of what can only be described as private military companies (PMCs), some of which grew larger and were even better equipped than the Tiger Force, because their principal purpose was that of providing 'shock troops' that lead offensive operations.[18]

Combatants of the BPM's 'Ba'ath Brigades' on the celebration of the 60th Anniversary of the (Syrian) Ba'ath Party, in April 2013. (SANA)

IRGC-QF's spearhead in Damascus: combatants of the Liwa Abu al-Fadl al-Abbas – Shi'a from Iraq and Lebanon, as seen in southern Damascus in 2012. (LAFA)

The quantitatively biggest para-military force upon which the officers of the IRGC-QF were able to call was the so-called 'Ba'ath Party Militia' ('Munazzamat Sha'biya', BPM). Through combining such formations with scattered detachments of the former regular military, raid squadrons of diverse intelligence and security services, and Shabiha gangs, the Iranians created a force modelled after the Basij Corps of the IRGC – officially designated the National Defence Force ('Quwwat ad-Difa al-Watani', NDF). In Hamedani's own words:

Some of the work we did was to create a popular force. At first they [Syrians] said, "you came here to create another army for us? Where is the money? Where are the weapons?" We said, "this is our strategy: the participation of the people to help the government in solving this crisis". When the role of these forces was established we saved Damascus with their help. They came and said that it must be put under the control of the army! We said that this is not correct. If you want to strengthen the army you must recruit forces. The first characteristic of the Islamic model and Basij thinking is that it is voluntary. This force is low-cost and lucrative. Really, they did not perceive this until they saw the results of these activities.'[19]

IRGC-QF's Para-State in Syria

The IRGC-QF never took care to convert the NDF into a coherent force, and thus it never established a centralised command system – because none was actually necessary: military operations of such formations were controlled from the IRGC-QF's own HQ, situated in the so-called 'Glasshouse' ('Maqare- Shishe'i'), outside Damascus International Airport (IAP). From there, Soleimani – followed by Hamedani, who replaced him in 2014 – not only exercised control of the military and intelligence apparatus, but of all major military operations run on behalf of the Assad government, and also began directing the process of integrating the IRGC-QF into Bashar al-Assad's Syria along the directive publicly expressed by Hojatoleslam Mahdi Taeb (one of the key planners of IRGC-QF's involvement in Syria) from 2013: 'Syria is the 35th province of Iran and it is a strategic province for us'.

Ever since, the IRGC-QF has exploited the fact that Bashar al-Assad has no other way of returning all the Iranian favours, or even pay for more troops other than those of the Republican Guards Division (RGD) and the Syrian Arab Air Force (SyAAF), but through signing numerous deals with IRGC-controlled commercial enterprises, granting them lucrative licences for mobile phone services and phosphate mining, the use of thousands of hectares of fertile land for farming, construction of oil and gas terminals, for electricity-generation and the rights to import electricity from Iran (via Iraq).[20] Furthermore, the Iranians have bought large parts of Damascus (including the entire former Jewish quarter), and began settling Shi'a from other countries there. Their clergy was granted the exclusive permission to open numerous religious teaching centres, such as in Damascus, Lattakia, and Jabla – all aimed at converting Sunnis and Alawis to 'correct', Shi'a Islam by ways of sermons and stipends.[21] Before long, the Iranians became frank enough to admit they are pursuing a long-term strategy in Syria. During the opening of a Shi'a mosque in Lattakia, one of their imams publicly announced to those who gathered: 'We don't need you. We need your children and grandchildren.'[22]

Unsurprisingly, related activities were actually an anathema in a country ruled by autocratic micromanagers of the 'Inner Circle' around Bashar al-Assad, and a group of hand-picked, senior military and governmental figures (so-called 'Confidantes'): from their standpoint, the entire state apparatus, including the nomeklatura, the military and security, and the Ba'ath Party, were maintained exclusively as an instrument of public control, while kept well away from decision-making bodies.[23] Nevertheless, Bashar, the Inner Circle and the Confidantes were still able to retain control because they oversaw more than 60 percent of whatever was left of the Syrian economy, all the nation's finances, and thus all the stocks of food, fuel, electricity, public transport, telecommunications, water supply, and fertiliser-supply. The distribution of such goods and commodities made them able to exercise control over diverse warlords – regardless if these generally preferred to follow the commands of IRGC-QF officers – and thus deeply encroached upon the government's autonomy and sovereignty. Indeed, because it realised that this organisation of armed forces fighting on its behalf was the only way for its own survival, whenever necessary, the Assad government went to lengths to suppress any kind of disagreement with related practices within the ranks of its own supporters. This went so far that some of its top military officers were 'disappeared' after Bashar officially declared Soleimani as 'the second most important person in Syria'.[24]

Finally, in 2016-2017, the IRGC-QF took care to formalise the status of the hodgepodge of militias it ran in Syria through forcing Damascus into officially declaring members of any of these as 'members of the Syrian armed forces'. In similar fashion, all the foreign combatants deployed in Syria under the control of the IRGC-QF were granted Syrian citizenship and also declared 'members of the Syrian armed forces'. Overall, the IRGC-QF has thus integrated itself within what is colloquially still known as the 'Assad government' to a degree where the two are inseparable: even should Bashar al-Assad ever be removed from power, the Iranians would still remain in a perfect position to maintain their position in the country.[25]

Due to the level of integration between Iranian-controlled militias and the forces of the Assad government, it often became nearly impossible to distinguish between them: top Iranian officials – like Major-General Soleimani – tend to describe them as the 'Axis of Resistance'. Correspondingly, and for reasons of simplicity, the military forces in question are going to be cited as 'Axis forces', in much of the rest of this narrative.[26]

Table 2: Basic Organisation of the Assad Governing System, 2012-2018

Figurehead	Official Military/Para-Military Organisation	Backer/Supporter
Bashar al-Assad	Republican Guards, Air Force Intelligence, al-Bustan Association	Makhlouf Clan, Russian Federation
Maher al-Assad	4th Armoured Division, Military Intelligence Branch, Hossn Association	IRGC-QF
Fahd Jassem al-Freij	Ministry of Defence, Syrian Arab Army, Syrian Arab Air Force, Ba'ath Party	IRGC-QF, then Russian Federation

'Second most important man in Syria' – at least until 2014: Major-General Qassem Soleimani. (FNA)

Solemani's closest aide and creator of the NDF-scam: Major-General Hossein Hamedani. (FNA)

CHAPTER 2
TOOLS OF WAR

Officially, the Russian military intervention in Syria began in September 2015, and then on a request by the Assad government. Officially, it is a legal intervention, run in accordance to widely-accepted international laws and norms, supported by the decision of the Russian parliament. Officially, it is a well thought-out, modern, professional expeditionary operation, carefully rehearsed in a series of military exercises run since 2012. Officially, it consists of air strikes against the IS, and deployment of Russian military advisors in support of the Assad government 'only': indeed, officially, the aims of this intervention are to 'fight the IS', 'stabilise the legitimate power' and 'create the conditions for political compromise'...officially, this intervention ended in November 2017 – although Moscow promptly left no doubt that its troops would remain based in Syria, 'permanently', too. With there being fundamental differences between what Moscow is doing officially and unofficially, and fundamental differences in the Russian style of warfare and that elsewhere, and most related accounts concentrating on the geo-politics of the intervention in Syria, this chapter is going to address the basics of the Russian strategic considerations and thinking, the military organisation, and then proceed with their tools: doctrine, strategy, tactics, equipment, capabilities, intentions, and related operations.

Boiling Point

In March 2015, the Jaysh al-Fateh (JAF) – a Turkish and Qatari-supported alliance of Syrian insurgents and transnational jihadists of the JAN – took Idlib (city). In April, it captured Jishr ash-Shughour. Shaken, even the IRGC-QF reached the decision to withdraw its forces from north-western Syria and concentrate on defending the Damascus and Western Aleppo areas only. Emboldened, the JAF continued its advance into north-eastern Lattakia and into the al-Ghab plain. Concerned over the prospect of losing its major port and the nearby Basel al-Assad IAP (the military side of which was officially designated Hmeimim Air Base), the Assad government rushed all the available troops into a desperate counter-offensive – only to suffer an entire series of disasters, in the period between June and September. This resulting crisis brought the situation within the Assad camp to boiling point: although surviving almost exclusively thanks to the IRGC-QF, the Inner Circle and Confidantes could not avoid the conclusion that they were about to fail even despite the Iranian military intervention. Furthermore, they began openly fearing the growing Iranian influence, as recalled by a Russian official who used to work in his country's embassy in Damascus:

> Assad and those around him are afraid of the Iranians... (there is) anger over the arrogance of the Iranians, who treat Syria like a colony...(they) mistrust Tehran's goals, for which Assad's position of power may no longer be decisive.[27]

Eventually, the Assad government would have been left without a choice but to request decisive help from Moscow.

An abandoned MiG-23MF interceptor (serial 2677) 'captured' when jihadists of the JAN and Jund al-Aqsa overran the Abu ad-Duhor AB, on 8 and 9 September 2015. Forces of the Assad government also lost the entire equipment of at least one SA-2 SAM-site, two intact MiG-21 interceptors, and two Mi-8 helicopters (including the serial number 1282) on that occasion. (JTF/HTS release)

Who called for Help?

Exactly when and in what form should Bashar al-Assad expressed his request for help from Moscow remains unknown. Official releases from Damascus and Moscow create the impression that this happened sometime in July 2015. On the contrary, Western sources have expressed strong doubt that this call was issued by the Assad government at all: one of the most-widespread publicly available versions is that a corresponding request was actually issued by Tehran – and then during multiple visits to Moscow by Major-General Soleimani.[28] Whatever the case was, one of the crucial conditions for the decision by the Putin government appears to have been related to the signature of the Iran nuclear deal in Vienna, Austria, on 15 July 2015 – the negotiations for which, apparently, included an agreement of Western powers to respect Iran's 'special interests' in Syria. Perhaps confirming such an agreement, Bashar al-Assad is known to have welcomed the signing of the JCPOA: indeed, he declared it, 'a great victory', and added that, 'we are confident that the Islamic Republic of Iran will support, with greater drive...' – him and his interests, of course.[29]

Myth of Russo-Syrian Alliance

The public impression created not only by the propaganda emitted by the Kremlin, but also that spread by the USA during the Cold War, is that Russia and Syria are tied through a close friendship going back for decades. A close study of related affairs reveals an entirely different picture. Certainly enough, Damascus did start buying weapons from the former USSR in 1955-1956, but only because Western powers repeatedly blocked its attempts to buy arms from elsewhere. Even then, and for most of the 1960s, Syria preferred to buy arms and advice from the former Czechoslovakia, because the quality of Czechoslovak products was considered better than that of the Soviet. By 1967, a government established itself in power in Damascus that officially declared itself as a 'Soviet ally' – yet never had more than 30 Soviet advisors in the country, nor bought any Soviet arms. Nevertheless, concerned about the increasing intensity of the Israeli attacks in April of the same year, Moscow warned Egypt of Israel preparing an invasion of Syria. Although finding no trace of evidence for the Soviet claim, Cairo reacted by mobilising its military and deploying it along the armistice lines with Israel, intending to lessen pressure upon Damascus. Subsequently, Moscow lost control of the situation, and this escalated to the point where Israel invaded Egypt on 5 June 1967, followed by Jordan and Syria, thus initiating the so-called 'Six Day War'. As a result of that conflict, ill-prepared Syria lost the Golan Heights. For the next six years, relations between Damascus and Moscow were 'tense' at best: Hafez al-Assad was a staunch anti-Communist, whose security services detained (and 'disappeared') thousands of Syrian leftists. This situation experienced a temporary change in 1973, when Assad acquired huge amounts of Soviet weaponry in order to enable his military to attempt recovering the Golan Heights, during the October War (also 'Yom Kippur' or 'Ramadan War') in the same year. However, in 1975, Moscow imposed an arms embargo upon Damascus because of differences of a political nature.[30]

Friendly relations were re-established in the period 1978-1981 when, concerned about the instability of the Assad government – which was facing a growing insurgency at home, and an Israeli invasion of Lebanon – Moscow deployed about 7,000 military advisors to Syria. This operation backfired: it prompted elements of the Syrian military into staging a coup, intended to be launched simultaneously with a popular uprising in Hama. Security services of the Assad government uncovered the plot and smashed the uprising, killing over 20,000 in the process. However, subsequently, the Syrian military was debilitated by massive purges: indeed, it never recovered its professional military capabilities again and, rather unsurprisingly, experienced another major defeat at the hands of Israel, during the fighting in Lebanon of June 1982. Following that experience, Moscow launched Operation Kavkaz-2, including the deployment of additional advisors and their own air defence units in Syria, but also advanced armament. However, while stabilising the position of the Assad government, this operation failed because the Syrian economy could not sustain another military build-up. On the contrary, in 1988, Moscow felt forced to withdraw all of its advisors from the country, and Damascus cancelled payments of its debts (most of which were related to massive arms purchases in the period 1967-1988) estimated at around US$13.4 billion. It was only 20 years later, in 2005 that relations between Russia and Syria were restored – primarily through the efforts of Vladimir Putin, who wrote off 73 percent of Syrian debts in an attempt to secure orders for the Russian defence and construction sectors. Even then, Damascus turned down most of the offers: although placing a few orders for overhauls of some of its military equipment, in 2008 it bought 33 old MiG-23s from Belarus instead of buying new aircraft from Moscow, and then cancelled all of the major contracts with Russian construction companies.[31]

Unsurprisingly, during the first year of the Syrian Crisis, Putin not only stressed there was 'no special relationship' with Damascus, but several times rebuked the Assad government, warning its days might be numbered and a ceasefire with insurgents was urgently necessary.[32] Although the Putin government did provide some support for the Assad government on the diplomatic level during the following years – for example through vetoing a total of four resolutions of the UN Security Council against Damascus, and

then effecting an agreement with the USA according to which the Assad government was to destroy its entire stockpile of chemical weapons – it was only following the West's reaction to the Russian invasion of Ukraine that Moscow seriously changed its position with regards to Syria. It did so not for the interests of Damascus, but for its very own interests, and even then: as of 2015, the Assad government was anything but 'friendly', and not even a 'reliable' partner of Russia.[33]

Presidents Assad (second from left) and Putin (third from left), during a meeting in Kreml in January 2005. (Government of the Russian Federation's release)

Reasons for the Russian Military Intervention

Considering all of the negative Russian experiences in Syria from earlier decades, one can't but wonder: how and why did the Putin government then decide to answer Assad's call for help positively, and thus wade into a conflict involving a myriad of competing factions, and including the risk of a military confrontation with the West?

Several times since 2008, Vladimir Putin, members of his government, and top ranks of the Russian military publicly stated that they consider Russia as in a state of a continuous proxy war with NATO, and the USA in particular. An important – though unspoken – motive behind such a standpoint is the threat posed by the rapid growth of Western economies for the Putin government. A prevention of the further expansion of Western influence thus became the principal reason why the Putin government launched a military intervention in South Ossetia against Georgia in 2008, and then invaded Ukraine and unilaterally annexed the Crimean Peninsula in 2014. From the standpoint of the Kremlin, the situation has only worsened ever since: the USA and its Western allies have reacted by subjecting Russia to severe embargoes, with crippling consequences for its economy and thus the entire population. Hemmed in, in urgent need of distracting its public, and of scoring propaganda points – also thought presenting itself as having recovered Russia's former status of a 'superpower' – the Putin government thus decided to divert the attention of the West through acting in Syria and thus, indirectly, breaching the international isolation: it aimed to decrease the Western diplomatic freedom of action, by curtailing its practical means of intervention.[34]

Moscow thus entered a long-term gamble, an outright game of poker: it put its bet on a factor in need of massive financial, logistical, and military commitment for years to come, without a certain outcome.

Strategic Planning

Strategic planning in Russia is run by the Security Council: this is an inter-ministerial body chaired by high-level officials (mostly with an intelligence and security background, similar to Putin's). While analysing their situation, and the situation of the Assad government, Putin and the Security Council sought to create a situation where the US and its NATO partners would not be needed in Syria. The logic dictated to them to secure supposed Russian 'military bases' in the country first, because this was certain to ensure that Moscow would retain a powerful part to play even in the case of any possible transition from the Assad government to another one. Moreover, from the standpoint of the Putin government and its top political and military aides, Syria was and remains related to the issue of securing a dominating position of Russia as the principal gas-supplier to the European Union (EU): already before 2011, and even more so ever since, the country was the 'missing link', a virtual 'hole' in a chain of gas-pipelines constructed in the Middle East and around the Mediterranean Sea, from Morocco in the west to Jordan in the east. Had this gap been closed – for example through a construction of a gas-pipeline connecting Qatar via Saudi Arabia and Syria to Turkey – the Russian de-facto monopoly on gas supplies to the EU would have been breached.[35]

Aware of the fact that the West was showing little desire for getting drawn into the war in Syria, Putin and the Security Council could have been certain that there would be no serious opposition to their intervention. On the contrary, the absence of consequent Western – and US in particular – policy had created a power vacuum not only in Syria, but in large parts of the Middle East, too, leaving Moscow free to use a combination of self-serving exaggeration, prevarication, bluster, and wilful projection of its own fantasies to 'impose' Russia as a major arbiter of power in that part of the World. Finally, the Russian defence sector, meanwhile in dire straits for many reasons (see below), could profit from the fact that the label 'combat proven' could be put on various of its products. Therefore, and like in Ukraine before, the Putin government opted for applying military force sparingly, in a mix of conventional and unconventional warfare, in a form that was promising to remain economic, and likely to score propaganda points – at home, and abroad.

Legal Background

From the Russian standpoint, the legitimacy of the military intervention in Syria is perfectly solid. Although the exact date on which such a request may have been issued remains unknown, sometime during the summer of 2015, the legal government of Syria – that of Bashar al-Assad – confirmed and legitimised in its position through democratic elections of 2014, issued an official invitation for a Russian military intervention in Syria. Following the internationally legal principle of 'intervention upon invitation', a corresponding military operation was then authorised by the Federation Council (Russia's upper house of parliament), on 30 September 2015.[36] Therefore, from the standpoint of Moscow, the Russian military intervention in Syria is run in accordance with valid domestic and international laws and regulations, and thus legal. This way of thinking is based on two legal principles: the legitimacy of the inviting authority, and the validity of the invitation.

The first ever 'multi-candidate elections' since the Assad clan established itself in power were held in Syria on 3 June 2014. The Putin government represents the standpoint that these elections were perfectly legal, and that they confirmed the legitimacy of the Assad government. Such argumentation roughly follows the following line: Article 2(4) of the UN charter dictates that all the states that are members of the UN shall refrain from the threat or use of force against the territorial integrity or political independence of any other member state. Correspondingly, any use of military force by one member state against another member state is illegal. There are only three exceptions from this rule: military action in self-defence, military action authorised by the Security Council, and military action based on 'principle of intervention upon invitation'. Therefore, and because the International Court of Justice tends to consider only those invitations to intervention to be legal that were issued by the legitimate governments, the Putin government insists that its intervention in Syria is perfectly legal – and that 'even' by Western standards.[37]

While beyond any doubt in the Kremlin, the legitimacy of the Assad government is hotly disputed – not only by the Syrian opposition and most Western powers, but even by a few well-positioned persons in Russia. The elections of June 2014 were boycotted by all the major opposition groups in Syria (including Kurdish militias), the entire population in parts of the country outside the governmental control (about 70 percent of Syria as of 2014), and excluded millions of refuges that had left Syria unofficially. This means that at least a third, if not a full half, of the electoral body in Syria did not participate, and thus never legitimised the government in Damascus. With the Assad government having a long and undisputed history of arbitrary arrest, bestial torture, prolonged detention, and systematic mass-murder of dozens of thousands of prisoners, in addition to violent restriction of the freedom of speech and the media, it is little surprising that the election results were dismissed by most of the international community.[38] Notably, at least some in Russia share such doubts too. Not only has Putin repeatedly cited 'mistakes' made by Bashar al-Assad, but in an interview with the US media, Chairman of the Russian Parliament's Defence Committee, Admiral Vladimir Komoyedov, stated about the Syrian president, 'The problem is that he has lost some of his authority.'[39]

Overall, because the people of Syria have never had an opportunity to freely elect their government, and their lives were in large part ruined by oppression through the actions of the Assad government, there remains a big question mark over the legitimacy of the same – and thus the legitimacy of its invitation for a Russian military intervention – and that 'even' by Russian standards.

Finally, the 'principle of intervention upon invitation' can only stand a legal basis if none of the resulting military action constitutes a violation of pre-emptive norms of international law. For example: according to Article 20 of the text 'Responsibility of States for Internationally Wrongful Acts' of the International Law Commission, air strikes on hospitals constitute a violation of the International Humanitarian Law (IHL). Therefore, should it turn out that the Russian military forces became involved in such attacks, Moscow's intervention in Syria would have no legal justification. This is the set of reasons why the Kremlin, the Foreign Ministry, and the Ministry of Defence (MOD) in Moscow have brushed all the related doubts aside and flatly denied any kind of violations of the IHL by Russian military forces in Syria, ever since 30 September 2015.[40]

Operational Planning

Traditionally, bridging the national security strategy and the military operational art in Russia is the Chief of the Russian General Staff (GenStab). As of 2015, this was Colonel-General Andrei Kartapolov: while a member of the Security Council, Kartapolov was also at the top of the chain of command of the Russian military – the GenStab. The body is staffed by a caste of professional planners that wear their own insignia, are never rotated through joint assignments, and thus never 'fixed' to a specific branch of arms. This is of particular importance because the GenStab has far wider authorisations and functions than, for example, its US-equivalent – the Joint Chiefs of Staff – while suffering from far less 'branch fixation'. Although having no operational control of the force, this body is responsible for planning at operational and strategic levels, works as a doctrine and capability developer – but also as equipment procurement authority.[41]

The primary origin of the GenStab's doctrinal thinking as late as of the early 2000s used to be World War II: related experiences were studied for decades by literally millions of Soviet and then Russian military officers. In comparison, Soviet and then Russian studies of conflicts like those fought in Africa, the Middle East, or South-East Asia of the last 70 years became foremost renowned for containing a mass of factual errors and nearly always omitting the key data. However, the – often painful – experiences from the Afghanistan War of the 1980s, but especially from Chechnya of the 1990s, have prompted a major change in the way the GenStab sees the nature of modern and future war. Its military theoreticians – foremost Major-General Ivan Nikolayevich Vorobyov (ret.) – have prompted multiple and fundamental reforms of the entire Russian military. The result is rather ironic: although the GenStab considers the local and regional conflicts as the most likely manifestations of war since around 2006-2008, it is still equipping and training the entire Russian military for fighting the most dangerous form of warfare: a large-scale, conventional war under nuclear-threat conditions. Nevertheless, in addition to depth, width, and height, the Russian military now considers the fourth dimension – information – as a fundamental element of warfare, and has identified the so-called 'indirect and asymmetric methods' and the general blurring of the lines between the tactical, operational, and strategic levels of operations as new components of warfare.[42] Therefore, the latest issues of the National Military Doctrine of the Russian Federation envisage military actions 'countering external dangers' (like the 'spread of international terrorism'), and the 'occurrence of sources of inter-ethnic/inter-faith tensions…and forcible extremism in various regions of the world'[43]

The exact degree to which the members of the GenStab have studied the situation of the Assad government and its military remain unclear. If they ever did something of that kind, they would have quickly drawn similar conclusions to those of independent military commentators in Russia, such as Lieutenant-Colonel Mikhail Khodarenok, who summarised along the following lines:

- The Assad government had no idea how to govern, nor even what was going on in most of its country; it had no stable sources of income and thus no money even for immediate defence expenditures.
- Military and security forces of the Assad government had mistreated the population to the point where they could not count on its support (not even of such minorities as Christians).
- The remnants of the military had no idea how to fight the war, no centralised command and control system, no reserves, and their commanders had no influence upon the distribution of supplies; indeed, whatever was left of the Assad government's military was suffering from endemic corruption, intrigues, and informal arrangements, resulting in troops that were ill-supported and ill-motivated to continue fighting.
- Only about 25,000 out of a nominal 120,000 troops of the Assad government were capable of fighting at all – and even these had not conducted a single successful offensive operation in over a year (as of 2015): for most of the time, they were engaged in extorting tributes from the locals at checkpoints.
- The actual fighting against opposition groups was done by the conglomerate of the IRGC, Hezbollah, diverse Iraqi and Syrian militias, and private military companies, all of which had their own interests.
- In turn, this meant that restoring the constitutional order would require a complete rebuilding of the military of the Assad government, combined with major diplomatic, political, economic, and propaganda efforts.[44]

Colonel-General Andrei Kartapolov, head of the GenStab as of 2015, and a member of the Security Council in Moscow. (Russian MOD)

Victory – by Air Power

Whatever the conclusions of Putin, the Security Council, and the GenStab were, what is certain is that the latter opted to run the military intervention in Syria in the form of three simultaneous operations:

- Establishing and securing the Russian military bases in Syria, and protecting these by their own, Russian, forces;
- Re-establishing and re-training the Syrian military with help of Russian advisors;
- Coercing the Syrian opposition into concessions.

While certainly concluding that the first two aims could be achieved through the deployment of a fairly limited contingent of the Russian ground troops and advisors, when studying possible options for the third, the GenStab opted for the application of airpower. There are multiple and very good reasons for the related decisions. In the view of the leading Russian military theoreticians, force is meant for coercion, rather than conquest, and it must be used cheaply, deniably when necessary, and with emphasis placed on retaining agility. Air power perfectly fits such a requirement. Moreover, diverse top Russian military commanders since the 1990s became obsessed with the idea of proving that their air force would be capable of winning wars on its own, the way *they think* the Western air forces have proven capable of winning wars in various conflicts of the last 30 years.[45]

Combined, such methods of operations were promising the military intervention in Syria to be run in a relatively cheap fashion, to end quickly, while scoring major propaganda points at home and abroad. In turn, an aerial campaign – combined with the growing presence of IRGC-QF-controlled militias – served the purpose of buying the time necessary to re-build the Syrian military, while limiting the prospects of the Russian forces suffering casualties and the Kremlin thus facing critique at home. That is how the primary tool of Moscow's gamble in Syria became their air power.

The State of Russian Air Power in 2015

The GenStab's decision to primarily use air power in Syria in turn implies the question about the status and capabilities of Russian air power as of 2015. There were – and there remain – giant question marks over this topic, and not for nothing. For the last 30 years, the predecessor of what since the same year is officially the VKS, has vegetated in shame. Massive losses of aircraft, personnel and facilities caused by the dissolution of the former Soviet Union, followed by massive budget shortfalls, resulted in its near-collapse in the mid-1990s. Preoccupied with necessary political and economic reforms, and lacking funding, Moscow was much too busy to even properly finance its armed forces: for much of this period, its military pilots were thus happy if they could get an operational aircraft and clock anything between 20 and 40 hours of continuation training annually. Serious tactical exercises and evaluations were run by a few instruction-research units only, and almost exclusively in cooperation with or on behalf of foreign customers.[46]

In 2007, the Putin government and the GenStab launched a major reform of the Russian military and defence sector. Known as the 'New Look', this had the primary aim of streamlining the former Soviet military and a bloated command structure into a modern and combat-ready force, and was accompanied with improved investment. The result was the VKS that began receiving a de-facto new generation of combat aircraft with much improved flying, range and payload-capabilities, while its crews began receiving serious military training again. Russian military pilots were once again proud – of themselves, their service, and their powerful aircraft, most of which are nowadays designed by the Sukhoi Design Bureau.[47]

Related reports have imposed a number of questions regarding non-quantifiable factors – like the quality of training, new developments of tactics and doctrine, leadership quality, and operational prowess. Classic examples were issues like the fact that during the times of the Soviet Union, the air force had no autonomous, but only supportive role. Furthermore, the idea of allowing flight leaders to make autonomous decisions was totally anathema to mainstream Soviet military thought: the GenStab was not only content but indeed determined to treat its fighter pilots as pawns. All decision-making was reserved for higher levels because Soviet commanders were convinced it belonged there. The question was therefore: did anything change in this regard? At least as important was the question of how would the VKS operate in such a scenario as in Syria? After all, this is a unique experience for the Russian air force: it had never before run an 'expeditionary' operation, far away from its borders. Moreover, while Russia had ground troops in Syria, its primary purpose during this intervention was not that of supporting these – which is the task for which the VKS and most of its equipment was envisaged – but that of achieving a political goal.

Some answers were obvious. The massive increase in fuel and spares-supply, and large-scale overhaul projects for available aircraft, but also orders for newly manufactured aircraft, have not only enabled the pilots to fly more often, and ground personnel to be trained more intensively, but have also enabled an outright revitalisation of the entire VKS. However, and despite obtaining new and much improved fighter-bomber types, the Russian air-space force still had no autonomous role. Since the reform, it exercised direct control only over the Long Range Aviation units, equipped with strategic bombers, and Military Transport Aviation, equipped with transport aircraft. All other assets – especially its tactical arm, the Frontal Aviation, equipped with fighter-bombers and attack aircraft, and the Army Aviation, equipped with attack, assault and transport helicopters – are operationally subordinated to the Joint Strategic Commands, i.e. front commanders, and used to support 'local' operational needs. Further down the chain of command, and following negative experiences from the Chechen wars, Russian regimental commanders had been given more freedom to decide independently how to conduct training and combat operations. Nevertheless, stolid conservativism continues to afflict training and tactics application until the time of writing, and safety remains a paramount issue – in turn curbing training methods.[48]

Other issues remained better hidden. For example, because of the often bombastic reporting by the Russian media – and the Western media developing the strong predilection for simply copy-pasting the same without any cross-examination – it remains largely unknown to the public that most of the reform of the defence sector (launched already in 2006) either never materialized, or was even reversed by 2015.[49] In particular, the Russian aerospace sector was already badly weakened by the Adolf Tolkachev espionage affair of the early 1980s (when Tolkachev revealed all the secrets about an entire generation of new combat aircraft and armament about to enter service to the CIA). It had never recovered from this blow before suffering the next: through much of the 1990s, thousands of highly skilled designers, engineers and nearly all of the skilled workforce either emigrated to the West or sought careers in other sectors. What was left of the Russian aircraft manufacturers was surviving by selling available designs and armament to export customers, while most other enterprises were limited to advertising paper projects or announcing new variants of already existing equipment – only a handful of which have ever seen the light of the day.[50]

The literal 'dot on the i' was the loss of dozens of high-technology enterprises in Ukraine, which were responsible for a mass of research and development projects. Even as of 2018, the Russian defence sector is still experiencing major problems in replacing the know-how, capabilities, and production capacities of the facilities in question. This crisis meanwhile reached such proportions that the Putin government and the GenStab were forced into the realisation that the Russian economy could neither support the necessary investment, nor could the defence sector deliver all the arms and equipment necessary for a complete upgrade of the military within the required period of time.[51]

Fighter-Bomber Fleet

At home in Russia it is the interceptors like the Mikoyan i Gurevich (MiG, meanwhile MIG RSK) MiG-31s that are at the forefront of the VKS' tactical component. In Syria the Russians needed fighter-bombers most of all. As of 2015, the backbone of the air force's fleet consisted of Sukhoi Su-27/30/35 (ASCC-code 'Flanker') single and two-seat fighters and fighter-bombers, including 53 Su-27SMs, 12 newly-built Su-27SM-3s, 70 legacy Su-27P/UBs (of which 36 were about to be upgraded to Su-37SM-3 standard), 60 newly-built Su-30SMs (about 20 of which were in service), and the first out of 48 Su-35S from an order dating back to 2009.[52]

The Su-35S is the ultimate single-seat, multi-role derivative of the original Su-27, designed to match generation 4.5 Western fighters, such as Eurofighter EF-2000 Typhoon and French-made Dassault Rafale. Featuring thrust-vectoring engines and much refined aerodynamics, it was to become the first in this – already third – generation of Flankers to receive a 'Russian-only' mission avionics and armament suite. However, its introduction to service was proceeding rather slowly because of a number of shortcomings and deficiencies revealed during the type's flight testing. Therefore, the most advanced of the aircraft in service with the VKS were Su-30SMs multi-role fighter-bombers. This is a derivative of the Su-30MKI/MKM exported to countries like Algeria, China, India, Malaysia and Venezuela, and roughly comparable to the Boeing F-15E in capabilities. Nevertheless, as delivered to the VKS, the Su-30SMs were still equipped with a French holographic HUD and a Russian avionics suite featuring Indian- and Israeli-made systems. The introduction to service of a

variant with 'Russia only' avionics suite in form of the Su-30SM-3 is still pending.

The advanced derivatives of the MiG-29 (ASCC-code 'Fulcrum') were to see only limited deployment in Syria, starting in 2017. While representing the quantitative backbone of the VKS, availability rates of remaining aircraft of this type are relatively low. Poor quality of mission avionics, short operational range, and severe fin cracks found on the majority of the remaining airframes prompted the GenStab to abandon the intention to proceed with a mid-life update to MiG-29SMT-standard. Similarly, a decision about an order for 30 MiG-35s, announced previously in 2013, has been repeatedly postponed, and the 'newest' examples still in service are 28 MiG-29SMTs and 6 MiG-29UBTs originally built through the installation of new avionics into airframes assembled in the late 1980s – destined for, but turned down by Algeria, in 2009.

Instead, the second of two backbones of the VKS' fighter-bomber fleet in Syria became the venerable Sukhoi Su-24Ms. As of 2015, there were two squadrons flying Su-24M2s and three flying Su-24M-SVP-24s. The Su-24 was always a handful to fly and maintain, and the type with the worst flight safety record in VKS' service. Therefore, Russian tactical aviation experienced a huge boost in its combat capabilities – at least in theory – when Moscow placed an order for 32 Sukhoi Su-34s (ASCC-code 'Fullback'), in 2008, followed by another for 92 additional such bombers, in 2012. Plagued by problems, the service entry was much postponed, and the type was declared operational only in 2014. Nevertheless, the 56 aircraft then enabled a conversion of four operational squadrons to the type, with further two following by 2018. There is little doubt that – thanks to its K-102 nav/attack system, V004 multi-function passive electronically scanned array, ventrally installed I255 B1/02 Platan laser- and TV-sight, and capability to haul up to 8,000kg (17.637lbs) of weaponry on 12 hardpoints over a combat radius of 1,100km (683 miles) – the Fullback is one of the most powerful tactical bombers anywhere around the World. Protected by the L265 Khibiny-MV self-protection electronic countermeasures suite and designed with potent stand-off and escort-jamming capabilities in mind, the type can to a certain degree match the capabilities of the Grumman EA-6B Prowler and Boeing F/A-18G Growler in regards of electronic warfare. However, it also proved a handful to maintain, susceptible to FOD and dust, and much too complex and inflexible to be deployed on a rapidly changing battlefield. Of course, it offers plenty of space for further upgrades, and there is little doubt that the VKS is going to continue to invest into it considerably. For example, the Su-34 is slated for adaptation with the – much delayed – Sych reconnaissance pod, thanks to which it should replace Su-24MR reconnaissance-fighters, which still equip four reconnaissance squadrons.

The final type the VKS was about to deploy in Syria was the Sukhoi Su-25 (ASCC-code 'Frogfoot') attack fighter. Designed as a subsonic, armoured fighter-bomber for close-air-support (CAS) to ground troops, the majority of about 140 aircraft still in service were manufactured in the late 1980s. However, due to low utilisation over the last 20 years, most still have plenty of service life ahead of them, and thus have been subjected to extensive overhauls and upgrade to Su-25SM/SM-1/SM-2 standard, since

2006. These sub-variants were still lacking the compatibility with guided weapons: this appeared only in the form of the Su-25SM-3 variant, which saw its premiere in Syria in 2017.

The primary air-to-air weapons of the Su-35s, Su-34s, Su-30s and MiG-29s deployed to Syria over the last three years are still the old R-27R/T (ASCC-code 'AA-10 Alamo') medium-range, semi-active-radar homing and/or Infra-red-homing missiles, and R-73E (ASCC-code 'AA-11 Archer') short-range, infra-red-homing air-to-air missiles, compromised to the West by Tolkachev already in the early 1980s. The often-idolised R-77/RVV-AE (ASCC-code 'AA-12 Adder') active-radar-homing, medium-range air-to-air missile was still not in service with the VKS, although undergoing low-rate research and development for more than 20 years, and widely exported. The original variant – R-77 – not only proved prohibitively expensive, but became rather notorious for suffering from poor manufacturing quality in service abroad. It was thus only on 26 August 2015, the GenStab (and thus the MOD) opened the tender to buy R-77s, and budgeted related expenses, with the intention to start acquiring such missiles in late 2016. Furthermore, while various new designs or further developments of the R-73 infra-red homing (IR-homing) short-range air-to-air missile (SRAAM) have been announced, none have entered service.[53]

The 'workhorse': the type that saw heaviest utilisation by the VKS in the first two years of the Russian military intervention in Syria is the Su-24M – about a dozen of which were always present at Hmeimem AB between September 2015 and late 2017. (Russian MOD)

Contingents of Su-25SMs deployed to Syria have varied in size: from 12 aircraft in September-October 2015, to only four for most of 2016 and 2017. This example was photographed while taking-off from Hmeimem AB in October 2015. (Russian MOD)

Helicopter Fleet

While the Russian Army used to operate its own flying branch as of 1990, this was re-integrated into the air force in 2003, since which time units equipped and trained to provide direct support for ground forces were subjected to the Army Aviation Department within the VKS' HQ.[54] The primary tool of this department is a large helicopter fleet, the backbone of which remains hundreds of old Mil Mi-8 (ASCC-code 'Hip') helicopters used for a wide range of tasks – from assault and CAS to utility and VIP-transport – and Mil Mi-24 and Mi-35M (ASCC-code 'Hind') attack helicopters/helicopter gunships. Projects for newly-designed attack and combat reconnaissance helicopters like the Mil Mi-28N (ASCC-code 'Havoc') and Kamov Ka-52 (ASCC-code 'Hokum'), originally developed in the late 1980s, had to be re-launched in the second half of the 2000s. With all the orders reported since 2005 totalling at 167 examples, the Mi-28N is meanwhile slanted to completely replace Mi-24s and Mi-35Ms. As of 2015, it was operated by six squadrons. On the contrary, the future of the Ka-52 did not look bright for a long time, until in 2011 Moscow announced a rather surprising decision to order 146 for delivery by 2020. Three squadrons were in the process of converting to this type as of 2015.

UAV Fleet

Although the Russian military theoreticians envisage the use of unmanned aerial vehicles (UAVs) in all sizes and for communications, intelligence, and electronic warfare tasks, in

A Su-30SM of the VKS, as deployed to Syria (note the armament consisting of R-27R and R-73 air-to-air missiles installed underwing, and two 250kg bombs installed under the intakes). As of 2015, this was the most-advanced multi-role fighter in Russian service. (Russian MOD)

The 'star': a Su-34 taking off from Hmeimem AB, armed with four FAB-500M54 bombs. (Russian MOD)

practice, the Russian military still primarily uses them as artillery spotters. Indeed, although the VKS was reasonably well-equipped with such systems as of 2015, even three years later it was still struggling to match the corresponding capabilities of its Western counterparts. The development of such platforms like medium-altitude long-endurance and high-altitude long-endurance platforms has proven to be literally 'mission impossible' for the Russian aerospace industry. Ironically, the VKS thus found itself without solution but to purchase a few Israeli Aircraft Industries Heron UAVs and launch licence production of these at home. Even so, neither Herons nor any other of about a dozen of tactical UAV types are capable of replacing the capability provided by old Su-24MRs, which are gradually being replaced by Su-34s. In turn, although the Russian aerospace industry successfully adapted several types of advanced navigation and targeting pods on Su-30MKI/MKMs manufactured for foreign customers, it is lagging in development of similar platforms for service with the VKS. None of these is expected to become available in significant numbers before 2020. Moreover, Russia still has no capability of deploying unmanned combat aerial vehicles.

Therefore, the branch that runs most UAV-related operations in Syria became the Russian Army. The Russian Navy added a small unit equipped with Forposts. Always understanding the requirement for well-planned and executed aerial (and ground) reconnaissance as vital for successful combat operations, this deployed a large number of home-made designs, including Elerons, Granats, Orlans, and Pchelas – all with maximum ranges of about 40 kilometres, and only capable of performing the most basic methods of artillery spotting (for example with the help of relative terrain features). Furthermore, because the first class of the army's UAV-operators was still undergoing training at the VKS' Academy (this began in 2013 and was about to be concluded in 2018), the army had to reach back upon officers from other branches, and with other specialities – foremost artillery – trained at the Russian Defence Ministry's Interbranch Centre for Unmanned Aviation in Kolomna. The primary UAV units in the Russian ground forces are UAV companies, one of which is usually assigned to each brigade.[55]

The first batch of VKS' Mi-24s deployed to Syria in August-September 2015 consisted exclusively of Mi-24Ps – a relatively old variant armed with a twin-barel GSh-30-2K 30mm cannon, attached to the right forward fuselage. (Russian MOD)

Other Reconnaissance Platforms

Being aware of the importance of electronic and signals intelligence, the VKS called upon its small fleet of Ilyushin Il-20M ELINT/SIGINT-gatherers (based on old Ilyushin Il-18 airliners) from one of the independent aviation reconnaissance

groups subordinated to the Main Intelligence Directorate (GRU). Later on, the strong cartographic traditions of the Russian military resulted in the deployment of one Antonov An-30 aircraft equipped for related purposes. However, more advanced reconnaissance platforms – like the Tupolev Tu-214R and Beriev A-50 SRDLO (Russian for 'Airborne Early Warning and Control System', AWACS) – were to follow only during the second phase of the VKS' deployment in Syria. One of the reasons is that such 'force multipliers' remain low in numbers. Only 17 out of 24 originally built A-50s were in service as of 2015, and these were insufficient to cover the immensely long borders of the Russian Federation. Furthermore, the fleet was still in the process of being upgraded to A-50U standard through the introduction of the Shmel-M radar and new, digital computing system. Even then, with the reported capability of tracking up to 150 targets out to a range of 600 kilometres (373 miles), the net effectiveness of VKS' A-50Us was rather comparable with legacy variants of the Grumman E-2C Hawkeye, meanwhile considered obsolete in the West, and largely withdrawn from service. Similarly, as of 2015, the VKS had only two Tu-214R-prototypes undergoing testing.[56]

One of the first photographs of an Il-20M of the VKS over Syria, taken on 5 October 2015 over Idlib (city). (Syrian social media)

An An-30 of the VKS as seen underway, high over Idlib province, on 12 November 2015. (Syrian social media)

Deployment

The first evidence for the presence of Russian Army troops in Syria appeared by early August 2015, when several BTR-80 IFVs were sighted onboard the Russian Navy ship *Nikolay Filchenkov* – an Alligator-class amphibious assault ship of the Black Sea Fleet – while passing the Bosporus. About a week later, at least one BTR-82A was captured on a video taken in north-eastern Lattakia during a counteroffensive run by the RGD and local militias in an attempt to recover some recently lost ground, during which Russian speaking combatants could also be heard. In reaction to such reports, the media controlled by the Assad government denied a possible Russian military intervention in Syria, even if confirming the presence of Russian military advisors in the Lattakia area: indeed, officials in Damascus continued their denials even when the first photographs of VKS aircraft and UAVs appeared in the social media on 1 and 2 September 2015. It was only a day later that reports about construction works at the Hmeimim AB surfaced – which received a new tarmac, a short taxiway, and housing for as many as 1,500 military personnel – that it became obvious that Moscow was in the process of becoming directly involved.[57]

On 7 September 2015, the first engineering units of the Russian military arrived at Hmeimim AB, to start the necessary work on reconstruction and expansion of this air base.[58] First reports about landings of at least two giant Antonov An-124 (ASCC-code 'Condor') transports were released by sources with links to various US intelligence services on 9 September 2015, and were followed by reports about direct involvement of the Russian troops in combat operations, a day later. Before long, it became known that the Russian military had about a company worth of T-90 tanks, 15 towed howitzers, 35 armoured personnel carriers, and at least 200 marines deployed in the Tartus area. Even then, Moscow commented that Russia was 'only' participating in the reconstruction of the Hmeimim AB, 'necessary for continuous military operations, deliveries of humanitarian aid and weapons purchased by Syria'. Along the same lines, Russian soldiers were 'only' guarding the 'airstrip and the delivery of goods', but 'not participating in any fighting'.[59]

Actually, while Hmeimim was still undergoing adaptation and expansion through the addition of the necessary housing and maintenance facilities, two further Russian amphibious ships and several transport aircraft had delivered the first battalion of the Russian Army, and a Pantsir-S1 SAM-site (ASCC-code 'SA-22 Greyhound') to Syria in the period 6-8 September 2015. With Hmeimim thus protected from air and ground attacks, the VKS began the process of deploying its combat aircraft, between the 15th and 18th of the same month. The first to arrive were four Su-30SMs, which were to serve as interceptors: they flew in a formation with two An-124s – which brought a pair each of Mi-8s and Mi-24 helicopters – and a single Ilyushin Il-78M tanker, via Iran and Iraq to Syria.[60] A day later, another formation followed along the same route, this time including a single Il-78M and five or six Su-24M2s. By 21 September – the day on which Damascus officially granted 'full access' to Hmeimim AB, 'and numerous airports around the country' – the number of VKS aircraft deployed at Hmeimim increased to 4 Su-30SMs, 12 Su-25s (these made a refuelling stop at Tabriz IAP, in Iran on their way to Syria, a day earlier), 12 Su-24s, and 12 helicopters (mostly Mi-24s), as listed in Table 3. Notable was that most of the aircraft and personnel were drawn from the Eastern Military District of the Russian armed forces, which in 2014 was one of the most active and best prepared: for example, VKS units assigned to that district had clocked an above-average number of flight hours (crews assigned to the 277th BAP, the Su-24M-unit of this district, flew 180 hours in that year; those of Su-25-equipped 187 GvShAP, flew 130 hours).[61]

On 22 September, the An-124s delivered additional elements of a Pantsir-S1 SAM-site to Hmeimim AB: the construction of corresponding facilities was detected by Western reconnaissance satellites a day later, by when a single Ilyushin Il-20M ELINT/SIGINT-gathering aircraft was sighted on arrival in Syria, too. With this, Moscow had all the elements it originally considered as necessary in place.

Table 3: VKS Aircraft Deployed in Syria, September-October 2015

Type	Borts/Registrations
Su-34[62]	20, 21, 22/RF-95818, 23/RF-95810, 25/RF-95811
Su-30SM[63]	26, 27, 28, 29
Su-25SM[64]	20, 21, 22, 23, 24, 25, 27, 28, 29, 30, 31, 32
Su-25UB	44, 53/RF-93055
Su-24M/M2/SVP-24[65]	04/RF-90943, 05/RF-90942, 06, 08/RF-90940, 16/RF-34007?, 25/RF-90933, 26/RF-90932, 71, 72, 74, 75/RF-90939?, 76
Il-20M[66]	
Mi-8AMTSh	212/RF-95585, 252/RF-95601
Mi-24P	02, 03/RF-91861, 21, 22/RF-91860, 23/RF-91864, 25, 30/RF-93571, 36, 37/RF-93062, 40/RF-91225

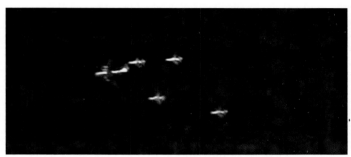

An Il-78 accompanied by four Su-24Ms, photographed high above eastern Homs, on 16 September 2015. (FSyA release)

Early Problems

Right from the start it was obvious that the Russian military intervention was an ad-hoc operation, launched in a great rush, under sometimes chaotic circumstances, without necessary preparations, indeed under conditions of significant political and military uncertainty – and urgency – and for reasons including outright megalomania. While most of this was openly confirmed by Moscow related reporting was virtually swept away by a rather ridiculous, but highly effective, propaganda campaign depicting a well-rehearsed operation, prepared for months in advance.[67]

Operational responsibility for the intervention in Syria was assigned to the Southern Military District (headquartered in Rostov-na-Donu), which in turn assigned the task to the HQ of the 58th Army of the Russian Ground Forces. Headquartered in Vladikavkaz (in the Republic of North Ossetia-Alania), and having fresh operational experiences from multiple conflicts in the Caucasus and in Ukraine in the period 2008-2014, the 58th Army was also exercising operational control of the 4th Air Force and Air Defence Army of the VKS. The first hurdle the 58th Army had to solve was the means of deploying thousands of troops, airmen and support personnel, and all the necessary arms and supplies to Syria. The shortest route between Russia and Syria leads via Turkey: as a NATO member, and then one of the foreign powers providing direct support for the opposition to the Assad government, Turkey could not be expected to let VKS' military aircraft make use of its airspace. Nevertheless, the Montreux Convention Regarding the Regime of the Straits, from 1936, grants the free passage for Russian warships and civilian vessels in peace through the Turkish-controlled Bosporus Straits and the Dardanelles. Correspondingly, the biggest part of the Russian military contingent, its heavy arms, equipment, supplies and ammunition was transported to Syria by the means of at least seven amphibious assault ships of the Russian Navy. However, all the combat aircraft, and most of the transport aircraft, had to take a route via the Caspian Sea, Iran and Iraq. Although nominally 'allied' with Iran, for unknown reasons Moscow had left its friends in Tehran in darkness over its intentions. Furthermore, there was great uncertainty over possible Western reaction: for example, the NATO – but especially US and allied forces involved in ongoing operations against the Daesh in Iraq – could have relatively easily imposed an aerial blockade of Syria. Moreover, it seems that Moscow was genuinely concerned that Lattakia and Basil al-Assad IAP/Hmeimim AB might be overrun by a sudden insurgent and JAN advance, before they would be ready to accept the planned deployment of the VKS. Therefore, all the combat aircraft transferred to Syria had their national markings and service insignia crudely over sprayed. Transport aircraft and/or Il-78M tankers escorting them carried English-language linguists who were the only persons permitted to maintain radio contact with air controls in Tehran and Baghdad. When questioned about the purpose of their overflights, they declared their aircraft as 'Syrian', i.e. in the process of being delivered to Syria.[68]

The next obstacle was that of basing of the Russian troops and airmen in Syria. As of July 2015, Russia had no military bases in Syria whatsoever. Certainly enough, Damascus granted Moscow the right to set up a naval depot inside the port of Tartus, in 1971: officially designated the 'Russia's Naval Force Sustainment Centre 720', this was never any kind of a 'military base', and hardly saw any use for the next 44 years: manned by exactly four Russian servicemen, it only saw occasional visits by vessels of the Russian Navy. In 2010, Moscow did ponder turning it into a full-blown base, but the Syrian crisis spoiled all the related planning: on the contrary, all the civilian staff were subsequently evacuated, and the Deputy Foreign Minister Mikhail Bogdanov stated that the depot had no strategic or military importance.[69] This issue was solved only on 26 August 2015, when representatives of the Assad government and the Putin government met in Damascus to sign 'The Agreement on Deployment of RF Air Force Group in the Syrian Arab Republic'. Valid for an indefinite period, this agreement specified the Bassil al-Assad IAP/Hmeimim AB with its infrastructure and the territory as provided for use by the Russian Federation at no charge.[70]

The next issues were those of the capacity and the vulnerability of Hmeimim AB, and surrounding Russian military installations. Constructed low on the narrow coastal plain, in the middle of an intensively cultivated area, and although having two runways, this facility lacked necessary ammunition depots and hardstands, and there was no space for any significant expansion of available

Соглашение
между Российской Федерацией и Сирийской Арабской Республикой
о размещении авиационной группы
Вооруженных Сил Российской Федерации
на территории Сирийской Арабской Республики

Российская Федерация и Сирийская Арабская Республика, именуемые в дальнейшем Сторонами,

руководствуясь положениями Договора о дружбе и сотрудничестве между Союзом Советских Социалистических Республик и Сирийской Арабской Республикой от 8 октября 1980 г., а также Соглашения между Министерством обороны Российской Федерации и Министерством обороны Сирийской Арабской Республики о военном сотрудничестве от 7 июля 1994 г.,

исходя из обоюдного стремления к защите суверенитета, территориальной целостности и безопасности Российской Федерации и Сирийской Арабской Республики,

признавая, что нахождение на территории Сирийской Арабской Республики российской авиационной группы отвечает целям поддержания мира и стабильности в регионе, носит оборонительный характер и не направлено против других государств,

подтверждая общность задач в борьбе с терроризмом и экстремизмом,

осознавая необходимость консолидации усилий по противодействию террористическим угрозам,

согласились о нижеследующем:

Page 1 of 'The Agreement on Deployment of RF Air Force Group in the Syrian Arab Republic', secretly signed in Damascus on 26 August 2015, but subsequently published by the authorities of the Russian Federation. (Pravo.gov.ru)

installations. Furthermore, it was well within the range of BM-21 artillery rockets and long-range artillery operated by multiple insurgent groups active in north-eastern Lattakia province. To make the issue of their security slightly easier, for at least the first week after their arrival, all the combat aircraft were parked in a long line down the eastern runway, clearly exposed in the open. Ahrar ash-Sham, one of the most powerful Islamist groups in Idlib and north-eastern Lattakia, wasted no time to 'declare a war on Russia', and launched a strike with BM-21s at Hmeimim AB on 21 September 2015. The VKS, the pilots of which were still preoccupied with settling down in Syria and flying orientation sorties, is said to have reacted with several air strikes. While such reports remain unconfirmed, if true, they would mean that the Russians flew their first combat sorties of this intervention a week before its official start, and before the necessary permission was granted – by Damascus and by the Federation Council of Russia.[71]

While officially Moscow never commented on even one of such attacks, they did not remain without consequences. Amongst others, the Russians felt forced to de-facto kick out the crews and helicopters of No. 618 Squadron, SyAAF, and construct them a new home-base roughly halfway to Lattakia, named 'Sanobar'. Foremost, an entirely new, well-fortified main ammunition depot for the VKS was constructed next to Istamo village, about five kilometres north of the main Russian air base. Furthermore, and until their engineers had completed the construction of protected positions for one S-300/400 and one Pantsr-S1 SAM-site each at Hmeimim AB, air defences of this facility had to be provided by the guided missile cruiser *Moskva*. Even then, the coverage of the Russian early warning radars deployed at Hmeimim was severely hampered by the Jabel an-Nusayriyah range: its average elevations of 1,200 metres above the sea level made it impossible for the VKS' radars to detect any kind of flying objects underway at altitudes below 6,000 metres as close as 40 kilometres north, and 15 kilometres east of the base – and that even if installed atop a 65 metres tall mast. This factor was to keep the Russian commanders in Syria on their toes for nearly two years.

The final hurdle for the Russian military intervention in Syria was that of sustaining the forces deployed in Syria: keeping them supplied for their mission. Until the time of writing, the major burden in regards of this effort is carried by amphibious assault ships of the Russian Navy running what became known as the 'Syria Express' in the West: a steady stream of supply runs from the Russian-controlled ports on the Crimea to the port of Tartus. However, urgent deliveries of specific equipment were carried out by transport aircraft – foremost An-124s and Il-76MDs, while personnel were transported by Ilyushin Il-62s and Tupolev Tu-154s. The majority of VKS' transport flights to Syria were starting at (and returning to) Krymsk AB; relatively few made stops at Sochi/Adler IAP, and some at Mineralnye Vody. Combat aircraft were usually flown to Syria from Mozdok AB.[72]

A still from a video showing the Ahrar ash-Sham's attack with BM-21 artillery rockets on Hmeimim AB on 10 November 2015. This insurgent group reportedly launched at least four such attacks in the period September-December of the same year: not one was ever commented upon by the Ministry of Defence in Moscow. (Ahrar ash-Sham release)

Group of Russian Federation's Forces in Syria

By 25 September 2015, the core of the Russian military mission to Syria was in position. The chain of command was running directly from the Kremlin to the MOD in Moscow, via the main headquarters (HQ) of the 58th Army in Vladikavkaz, to HQ of the 'Group of Russian Federation's Forces in Syria' (GRF) at Hmeimim AB. The latter found itself in control of a group of about a dozen of battalion-sized task forces of ground troops, and an artillery group, which were in the process of deploying at various hot-spots (see Table 4), but also the 'Training Mission to the Syrian Arab Army', including several teams of Russian officers that served as advisors for diverse military units and militias loyal to the Assad government. However, the primary tool of the 58th Army's combat operations became known as the 'Aviation Group of the Russian Federation in Syria'. Ever since September 2015, this

consisted of two regiment-sized formations: the fighter-bomber wing, and the helicopter wing. Initially, the fighter-bomber wing included 32 combat aircraft, supported by a single Il-20M. The helicopter wing initially included a total of 14 helicopters.

Table 4: Ground Units known as assigned to the GRF, September 2015–February 2016

Unit	Base or Area of Operations	Notes
HQ GRF	Hmeimim AB	
Security Element		1 battalion in total
3rd SPETSNAZ Brigade	Hmeimim AB	1 company
22nd Guards SPETSNAZ Brigade	Hmeimim AB	1 company
Perimeter Defence		
810th Naval Infantry Brigade[73]	Tartus	542nd Assault Battalion
SF Group		advisors and FAC
16th SPETSNAZ Brigade	Lattakia	1 battalion
24th SPETSNAZ Brigade	Aleppo	1 battalion
Senezh Brigade	Hmeimim AB	1 sniper team
7th Guards Assault Division	Palmyra	162nd Reconnaissance Battalion
Electronic Warfare Brigade		
66th Signal Brigade	Hmeimim AB	1 company
17th Electronic Warfare Brigade	Hmeimim AB	1 company, 4 1RL257 Krashuha-4 EW systems
64th Motor Rifle Brigade	Hmeimim AB	6 R-330B UHF-jamming systems 3 R-378 HF-jamming systems 6 1L29 SPR-2 Rtut-B radio-proximity-fuse jamming systems
UAV Unit[74]	Hmeimim AB	Orlan-10s & Forposts
Military Police		
130th (Ind.) Moscow Brigade	Hmeimim AB	1 battalion
Ground Units		
27th Guards Motor Rifle Brigade	southern Aleppo	1 tank company (T-90s), 2 motor rifle companies; about 320 troops
28th Motor Rifle Brigade	Hama	battalion-sized force, deployed in November 2015
32nd Motor Rifle Brigade	Hama	battalion-sized force, deployed in November 2015
34th Motor Rifle Brigade	Tartus	battalion-sized force, deployed in November 2015
74th Guards Motor Rifle Brigade	Hama	battalion-sized force; about 440 troops
336th Naval Infantry Brigade	Khelkhleh AB, Suwayda AB	protecting ELINT/SIGINT-bases operated by the GRU
Artillery Group		
8th Artillery Regiment		6 MSTA-B howitzers
20th NRBC Regiment		6 TOS-1A MRLS
120th Artillery Brigade		18 MSTA-B howitzers

Unit	Base or Area of Operations	Notes
439th Guards Rocket Artillery Brigade		4 Smerch MRLS
Aerospace & Missile Defence Group[75]		
S-400 Battalion	Hmeimim AB	1 SAM-site, arrived 26 Nov 15
S-300 Battalion	Hmeimim AB	1 SAM-site, arrived 24 Sep 15
Buk-M2 Battalion	Hmeimim AB	1 SAM-site
Pantsir-S1 Battalion	Hmeimim AB	1 SAM-site

Target Selection

With all the necessary assets and supplies in place, the question was that of how, and against whom, would the VKS operate in Syria. Indeed, for most of the first two years of the Russian military intervention in Syria, one of the biggest 'mysteries' about the VKS' methods of operations was that of targeting selection – one of the most crucial elements in warfare: in order to destroy its targets, any military force needs to know what these are, and where they are. Nominally, such information is supplied by military intelligence, which in turn depends on open-source (OSINT), optical, communications, electronic, and signals intelligence (COMINT, ELINT and SIGINT). Unsurprisingly, the Russian military places heavy emphasis on careful reconnaissance. However, on its arrival in Syria, the commanders of the GRF had no trace of clue about what was going on, or where, nor about who-was-who in the war.[76]

A cross-examination of some of the related information released in the Russian media, with information provided by sources in Syria, has meanwhile revealed that the target selection of the GRF – and thus its VKS' element – was quite straightforward. Although Moscow boasted about deploying 10 reconnaissance satellites in the space above Syria, only those equipped with electro-optical means of reconnaissance have proved of serious use, and even then: their photographs could be downloaded only two times a day. Some battlefield reconnaissance was provided by UAVs and, certainly enough, the MOD in Moscow even claimed that these would represent the primary means of targeting-intelligence.[77] However, due to the short range of the available platforms, they were unable to provide sustained coverage. Thus, for most of the first year of combat operations, the majority of the critical targeting intelligence was supplied by the intelligence services of the Assad government. It took nearly a year for the VKS HQ in Hmeimim to build up its own intelligence picture of the battlefield, primarily collected with help of ELINT/SIGINT operations of the sole Il-20 deployed in Syria, and UAVs.[78]

The resulting reliance on intelligence provided by dubious sources, or gathered from the immediate frontlines was not only to cause lots of problems with regards to combat operations, but foremost to have grave consequences for thousands of civilians living in parts of Syria controlled by insurgents. Namely, the Assad government was most keen to destroy its direct competition: about 400 so-called 'local councils', civic authorities that ran the everyday life in parts of Syria controlled by the opposition, nearly half of which were meanwhile elected in relatively 'primitive', even if 'free' elections. No matter how much ignored by Western decision-makers, media, and public in general, their sheer existence

was an undeniable proof that the Syrians are perfectly capable of self-administering themselves in a civilised – and pluralist – fashion, without turning into hordes of blood-thirsty jihadists, and that the Assad government was actually surplus. In the perfect tradition of authoritarian ways of fighting insurgencies, and in order to disrupt the work of such authorities, Damascus ordered the SyAAF into attacks on hospitals, bakeries, food storage sites, water-supply, and similar facilities in insurgent-controlled areas already by mid-2012.[79]

The Russians decided to follow the pattern, partially because they did not know any better; partially because it's an element of their own strategy for conflicts of this kind; partially because it was suitable for their intention to distract, divide, demoralize, and eradicate all forms of government and civil society competing with the Assad government; but also because of their obsession with the 'continuous proxy-war with the USA'. The latter factor is known to have prompted the GenStab in Moscow, and thus the HQ of the 58th Army, and that of the GRF, to aim for an annihilation of US-supported insurgent groups: civic authorities supported by Western governments and non-governmental organisations were sorted into the same class, or declared as 'terrorists'. Obviously, both sorts of target were very much in the interest of the Assad government, the security services of which knew that it was such civic authorities, and such insurgent groups – and not transnational jihadists – that were its most dangerous and effective enemies on the battlefield. When all these aims were combined, they resulted in the creation of a rather sadistic kind of map of Syrian battlefields: areas controlled by the opposition were painted in green, and declared as 'controlled by the JAN' or 'by terrorists'; those controlled by the Daesh were painted in black. The population in both types of zones were then 'warned' to leave by announcements in the media and through leaflets, and then everything in these areas was declared as 'legitimate targets'. Certainly enough, the pilots of the VKS were indoctrinated correspondingly – by an explanation that all the targets had been carefully sorted out by their HQ – as one of them summarized:

> We drop weapons only on the coordinates that come from the headquarters and, therefore, have already been clarified. Therefore, if I strike, I am sure: this is a blow to terrorists.[80]

A Su-24M of the VKS releasing an OFAB-250-270 high-explosive fragmentation (or 'general-purpose') bomb from an altitude of about 6,000 metres upon a 'target' in the Idlib province in late 2015. Regardless of how imprecise, these aircraft and such weapons were to become the primary means of the Russian campaign against the native insurgency in Syria. (Russian MOD)

A staged photograph showing a 'pilot disembarking a Su-25SM' of the VKS at Hmeimim AB (note that the pilot is wearing no g-suit). (Russian MOD)

Tactical Planning

At least since the October 1973 Arab-Israeli War, the fundamental principles of the former-Soviet, and then the Russian, aerial warfare are the moment of surprise, strict centralisation of command and control of all operations, and dependence on advanced, ground-based air defences.[81] The VKS adopted most similar principles and sought to operate accordingly during the intervention in Syria.

For the purpose of exercising tight, centralised command and control, it deployed one *Panorama* mobile command post (CP): this is an automated support system for command, control, and communication, compatible with a wide range of components, different software, and communication systems, that acts as the air defence HQ at Hmeimim AB. Using electro-optical cables, the Panorama CP in question is linked to a Kolchuga electronic support measures (ESM) system, a Krasuha-4 electronic warfare system (used for countering airborne early warning and control systems, AWACS), manned interceptors and surface-to-air missiles: the resulting 'integrated air defence system' (IADS) is linked with help of a Polyana automated tactical management system (ATMS) that serves the purpose of coordinating the work of all the integrated elements.[82] Additional advantages of the close integration of the VKS element with the unified command of the GRF at Hmeimim was that it made it easier for the commanders to coordinate aerial operations with those of the artillery. Finally, Russian commanders generally prefer to execute a previously rehearsed mission that fulfils the mission requirements adequately, than to attempt planning and executing a custom planned mission that fulfils the mission perfectly. They prefer to sacrifice flexibility for speed in planning and execution. It is because of this that automated command and control systems are much appreciated.[83]

Correspondingly, all the planning for combat operations was (and still is) run by the HQ GRF. Initially, the majority of air strikes were delivered on targets chosen at between 12 and 48 hours beforehand, at designated times – along so-called 'daily tasking orders'. Because of the complexity of the nav/attack equipment of types like Su-24, Su-30, and Su-34 in particular (specifically: the avionics of the Su-30SM needs at least 30 minutes to 'spool up', programming of a single mission into the nav/attack system of Su-24 often takes longer than an hour), lengthy preparations for their combat sorties were necessary. Therefore, but also in order to offer as many of its crews the 'taste of combat' as possible, the VKS deployed two flying crews and two ground crews for every aircraft of these types to Hmeimim AB, enabling its machines not only to be turned around more quickly, but also to be flown into repeated operations always operated by a fresh crew.[84] Its pilots and navigator/bombardiers were given the necessary time for a thorough preparation, selection of armament, methods of attack, manoeuvres in the vicinity of the target and other key tactical options, but – at least initially – had been assigned directions and heights of target approach.

CHAPTER 3
INTO ACTION

Officially, the first Russian air strikes in Syria were flown on 30 September 2015, when the VKS launched a total of 20 sorties. Early in the morning, a pair of Su-24Ms bombed a base of the Jaysh at-Tawhid (affiliated with the Free Syrian Army, FSyA) in the Rastan-Talbiseh Pocket (RTP), north of Homs. This attack was followed by bombardments of Talbiseh and Zafaraniya in the same area. A pair each of Su-24s and Su-25s then bombed the HQ of Tajamu al-Azza (another FSyA affiliated group, vetted by the CIA and equipped with TOWs) in northern Hama, while a pair of Su-34s bombed the HQ of the 24th Division FSyA in at-Tilol al-Hmer, near Qunaitra, in south-western Syria. Eight additional air strikes were flown the following night: all by Su-24Ms and Su-34s. The majority – up to 90 percent – of these early strike sorties were relatively straightforward: flown by day-light, they consisted of a take-off, climb to safe altitude, flight straight to coordinates provided by the mission-tasking cell, an automatic bomb release on pre-selected geographic coordinates, and return to base. Average duration of each such mission was about 45-60 minutes.

Lies in the Air

Reporting about early air strikes of the VKS by various officials in Moscow was not only confusing or controversial but often outright absurd. The MOD announced that all attacks had hit, 'objects of the Islamic State in Syria', and the Chief-of-Staff of the Russian Army, Lieutenant-General Sergey Ivanov, stressed that, 'Russia will only use its air force in Syria against the Islamic State terrorist group'. Furthermore, he added that, 'no ground troops will be sent'. While both were in line with the authorisation provided by the Federation Council on the same day, such statements were an obvious lie, because not one of the air strikes had hit Daesh, and by 10 October 2015 up to 5,000 Russian Army troops were not only deployed in Syria, but involved in ground operations, too.[85]

That was only the start of the controversy, the more different officials in Moscow raced to contradict each other over the aims and scope of the military intervention in Syria, the more the situation resembled scenes from assorted Keystone Cops movies of the 1920s. For example, while the Russian Foreign Minister Sergey Lavrov flatly denied accusations that air strikes were aimed at targets other than Daesh, Putin's spokesman Dmitry Peskov explained that Moscow was targeting '…organisations…chosen in coordination with the armed forces of Syria', adding that these were 'Islamist extremist organisations… supported by the CIA'.[86] Indeed, while on 2 October 2015 the MOD claimed, 'an air strike on IGIL in Ma'arat an-Nauman' (Idlib) – where there was no Daesh, *ever* – only a day later, the Chief of the GenStab, Colonel-General Andrei Kartapolov, left no doubts about the priority in the VKS' targeting, when publicly 'recommending' his 'US colleagues', to, '…withdraw from Syria all valuable individuals trained with US taxpayer's money…'. With this, it became clear that the primary target of the Russian operation would be insurgent groups supported by the US and its allies, and other 'Western interests in Syria' – including civic authorities in insurgent-controlled areas – and that irrespective of the fact that attacking such groups was in turn strengthening the position of all the possible extremists.[87]

In Damascus, this controversy grew even bigger considering the fact that the Russian air strikes were hitting positions of FSyA-affiliated groups at the time troops still loyal to the Assad government were besieged by Daesh at Kweres AB, east of Aleppo; in the city of Dayr az-Zawr and at the local military bases; and at the time the town of Palmyra and all the gas and oilfields of eastern and central Syria were under the control of the extremists: indeed, at the time transnational jihadists of the JAN, and Syrian Salafists of Ahrar ash-Sham were only 21-26 kilometres from Hmeimim AB.[88]

Irrespectively of the actual situation on the ground, the Russian air strikes went on in the same style on 1 October, when VKS re-attacked several targets in the RTP and northern Hama, claimed as 'destroyed by precise hits' the previous day. Unsurprisingly considering the resulting exchange of accusations and counter-accusations between the East and the West that was to follow, it remained unknown that one of VKS' Su-25 was damaged by ground fire (apparently a MANPAD) while underway over the al-Lataminah Salient in the northern Hama province, or that during the evening of 1 October, Russian bombs killed at least three civilians (including a five-year-old girl) and injured 12 others in Habeet. Apparently, the damaged Russian fighter-bomber managed to return to Hmeimim AB without further incident. As far as can be assessed from hundreds of videos and photographs taken during the following weeks – and unsurprisingly considering the fact that safety remains a paramount issue for the VKS – the result of this experience was that fighter-bomber crews were subsequently prohibited from descending below altitudes of between 4,500 and 6,000 metres (roughly 15,000-20,000ft), where they remained outside the reach of the MANPADs.[89]

Selection of Weapons

The VKS continued bombing similar targets during the following days, only to spark another controversy – this time in regards of weapons it was deploying. The MOD in Moscow and the Kremlin-controlled media have emphasised the widespread use of so-called precision guided munitions (PGM), including diverse guided bombs and missiles. Correspondingly, Su-34s were demonstratively shown while armed with brand-new KAB-500S-E GLONASS (globalnaya navigatsionnaya sputnikovaya systema' or 'global navigation satellite system') guided bombs, KAB-500Kr TV-guided bombs, and KAB-1500LG laser-guided bombs (LGBs) with 24N1 gimballed semi-active laser-homing seekers. Indeed, even Su-24Ms were shown while armed with old guided missiles like Kh-25 (ASCC-code 'AS-10 Karen') and Kh-29 (ASCC-code 'AS-14 Kedge'). However, a simple matter of fact is that while equipped with a reasonably large number of aircraft compatible with PGMs, the Russian air force lacks the stocks of guided weapons necessary for their widespread application. This is an issue related as much to the low stocks of guided weapons inherited from the USSR, as to the high price of new PGMs, to the training standards within the VKS, and to the loss of links to defence sector of Ukraine.[90]

As the following weeks were to show, between 95 and 97 percent of weaponry deployed by the VKS in Syria consisted of assorted types of free-fall bombs, primarily armed with high-explosive incendiary warheads, but also of highly controversial, so-called cluster-bomb units (CBUs). Obviously, when released from altitudes at which the VKS fighter-bombers usually operated (4,000 metres/13,123ft), the precision of unguided weapons is abysmal by modern-day standards. This did not change even when the Russians attempted to saturate each of their targets with between two and four 250 or 500 kilogram bombs – first released by pairs of aircraft, and then by additional formations – and then ordered their crews into repeated strikes on the same targets, all in attempts to finally destroy these.

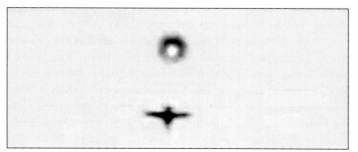

A still from a video showing a hit on a VKS Su-25 over northern Hama on 1 October 2015. (Syrian social media)

A FAB-500M-62 general purpose bomb on a trolley underneath a Su-34 of the VKS at Hmeimim AB, in October 2015. (Russian MOD)

A Su-25SM starting from Hmeimim AB armed with four FAB-250M-62 general purpose bombs. (Russian MOD)

VKS' technicians installing OFAB-250-270 high-explosive fragmentation bombs on a Su-34. (Russian MOD)

Ground crews running checks on a Su-34 armed with (from left to the right) R-73 and R-27R air-to-air missiles, KAB-500Kr TV-guided bomb (inboard underwing pylon), and a FAB-250M-62 general-purpose bomb under the intake. (Russian MOD)

A still from a video showing two VKS technicians in the process of arming fuses of an OFAB-250-270 high-explosive fragmentation bomb on a Su-24M. (Russian MOD)

This still from a video released by the Russian Ministry of Defence clearly shows a Su-34 of the VKS rolling for take-off from Hmeimim AB while hauling a load of four RBK-500SPBZ-D cluster bomb units, on 3 October 2015. (Russian MOD)

A Su-34 of the VKS seen while releasing a KAB-500S-E GLONASS guided bomb, supposedly over Raqqa, in early October 2015. Although such occasions were highly publicised by Moscow, the total number of PGMs deployed by the VKS over Syria can be counted on the fingers of two hands: the majority of targets they may have hit remain unknown until today. (Russian MOD)

Another still from a video released by the RT showing front parts of two RBK-500 CBUs installed on a pair of MBD3-U6-68 multiple ejector racks within the 'funnel' between the intakes of a VKS Su-34 at Hmeimim AB, in October 2015. (Russian MOD)

SVP-24 Legend

The MOD in Moscow reacted by launching the legend, according to which the use of the Gefest & T SVP-24 digital nav/attack system on VKS' Su-24s and Su-25s (and, later, on, on Tupolev Tu-22M-3 bombers) would make these capable of delivering unguided bombs with a degree of accuracy comparable to that of guided bombs.[91]

SVP stands for 'specialised computer subsystem' ('spetsializirovannaya vychislitelnaya podsistema'): it is a digital upgrade package aimed at improving the flexibility and precision of the nav/attack system of the Su-24M fighter-bomber. First applied during the overhauls and upgrades of Algerian Su-24MKs, in the period 2001-2006, it quickly proved more economic than the Sukhoi's own project, officially run under the designation Su-24M2. Correspondingly, while only about 28 VKS aircraft (a total of two squadrons) were upgraded by Sukhoi, by late 2014, Gefest had installed the SVP-24 into about 60 Su-24Ms.

The essence of the SVP-24 is the GLONASS-supported PNS-24M nav/attack system, coupled to the KAI-24P head-up-display (HUD), the SV-24 mission computer, the OR-4TM liquid crystal displays (for the RWR, the terrain-following radar, the Kaira-24 laser-ranger and marker; and for the flight/weapons/navigational data), the SRNS-24 navigation system, the UVV-MP input/output device ('keyboard') and the TBN-K-2 flight recorder.[92] The most obvious net results of the entire effort was that it became easier for crews to program the nav/attack system within less than one hour, enabled them to manoeuvre their aircraft within the last minute before weapons release, and provided them with similar HUD-symbology to that available on all Western fighter-bombers equipped with so-called CCIP-computers that have entered service since the mid-1970s. A less obvious result was that the SV-24 could be pre-programmed for automatic weapons release; indeed, for automatic weapons release on the basis of data provided from the ground only after the aircraft took-off, as will be discussed below.[93] Unsurprisingly, in operational service in Syria, the SVP-24 proved anything other than enabling some sort of mythical precision: video-evidence released by the MOD in Moscow in early October 2015 had shown that VKS' bombers equipped with the SVP-24 were usually missing their targets by 100 metres.

First Improvements

With hindsight, it is certain that the MOD in Moscow did not believe its own propaganda. On the contrary, already during early October 2015, it introduced a series of measures aimed at improving the precision of VKS' air strikes.

The first of these was the appearance of so-called 'forward air controllers' (FACs) – usually pilots or other military flying personnel that underwent specialised training. Since 2012, Russian FACs were equipped with the Metronom command and control system – the first element of network-centric warfare introduced to the Russian military. This includes range-finding, GLONASS-supported binoculars, used to acquire target coordinates, linked to a ruggedized tablet computer: with the help of this equipment, and the R-853-V2M radio, the FAC can forward standardised target information (including target type, fortification level, air defences and similar details) either to the battalion command post, or directly to the aircraft. Starting from mid-October, each

of about a dozen of the battalion-sized task forces of the Russian Army deployed in Syria was assigned one FAC-team. Whenever the battalion commander authorised the request for air support, the coordinates were forwarded to the nearest aircraft equipped with the SVP-24 system: the coordinates were automatically fed into the nav/attack system of the aircraft, which then generated flight direction commands for the crew to follow until a targeting solution was achieved. Bombs were then delivered on the provided coordinates, without the necessity for the crew to ever acquire any of the targets with on-board systems.[94]

During the first six months of the Russian military intervention in Syria, the FACs were serviced by about 10-20 percent of combat sorties flown by the VKS. The aircraft in question were either held at 5-15 minute readiness on the ground at Hmeimim AB, and then launched on request from forward air controllers, or took-off and then orbited pre-determined areas until provided with targeting data. The primary type used in this fashion was the Su-24M/SVP-24, because it was equipped with the Metronome communications and information management system that allowed data-targeting coordination with help of automated upload from the ground – directly from computers carried by FACs, and without involvement of the HQ at Hmeimim AB.[95] One of the Russian FACs explained his methods of operations as follows:

> I usually pick a location with a good overview of the area. Most often, I'm working with crews of Su-24s. Of course, with helicopter pilots too, and crews of other aircraft. With helicopter crews, I usually communicate with the radio. But, when cooperating with aircraft, it's different: I can use special equipment to provide target coordinates directly to the aircraft. Everything is quick and easy: from my point of view, it's simple…[96]

In this fashion, the VKS began introducing the so-called 'network-centric warfare' to its methods of warfare.

However, while the target coordinates provided by the FAC have enabled the VKS to provide reasonably effective close air support (CAS) to their own and allied troops, they failed to improve the precision of air strikes run with help of SVP-24 nav/attack systems. One of the reasons was the degenerated state of the entire GLONASS system, caused by the lack of funding in the 1990s and 2000s. Certainly enough, the restoration of the system was made one of the top priorities of the Putin government, and related funding was significantly increased (consuming up to a third of the budget of the Russian Federal Space Agency as of 2010-2011). However, the recovery of the system was rather slow: it had achieved 100 percent coverage of Russia's territory by 2010, and then the full global coverage by 2011-2012, but most of the satellites were still in need of replacements and upgrades, and the related work still very much going on as of 2015. The result was that at peak efficiency, the standard-precision signal was insufficient for military purposes. Therefore, the VKS began deploying so-called differential correction stations along the battlefields in north-eastern Lattakia, starting in mid-October 2015. These simple devices had the purpose of augmenting and correcting signals from GLONASS satellites in order to improve the accuracy of the entire system. Through the combination of

A VKS Su-24M armed with four FAB-500M54 bombs taking off from Hmeimim AB for a strike sortie on 3 October 2015. (Russian MOD)

A still from a video showing a fully-equipped Russian FAC on the frontlines in northern Lattakia, in April 2017. (Russian MOD)

all these methods, the VKS has eventually managed to improve the average precision of its air strikes to between 30 and 40 metres, which was considered sufficient enough. Perhaps more importantly, the improved GLONASS coverage has enabled more complex routing of VKS' aircraft, in turn enabling air strikes from unexpected directions.[97]

With such improvements in the back, and Moscow keen to propagate the story of doing more against Daesh than the US-led coalition did, the Aviation Group at Hmeimim received the order to deploy single aircraft into attacks on multiple targets during the same sortie: correspondingly, even famed Su-30SMs – deployed to Syria for running air defence operations – were loaded with unguided bombs of 250 and 500 kilograms.

IV Assault Corps

In the meantime, the Russian officers of the Training Mission to the Syrian Arab Army were working feverishly on re-establishing some semblance of a regular armed force for the Assad government.

Finally realising that the famed 'NDF' was actually a hodgepodge of sectarian militias and criminal gangs – some of which were either operating independently from the government or even fighting it – and that the Assad government was in control of no more than 6,000 fighters both 'capable' and 'loyal' to it, they first reacted with a suggestion to axe all the militias.[98] The combination of resistance from Maher al-Assad and the IRGC convinced them that the time was not yet ripe for such ideas. Therefore, they began mixing whatever was left of regular units with diverse militias, thus creating the IV Assault Corps.

The IV Assault Corps was perhaps the best example for the status of the 'military' fighting 'for Assad' as of 2015. It consisted of two major groups. One was centred on the 103rd Brigade RGD, reinforced through the addition of the Liwas Suqour as-Sahra and Dir as-Sahel (the latter commonly declared as the 'Marines' 'Naval Commandos' or even 'SEALs' of Syria), an unknown battalion equipped with T-72s, the 46th Armoured Battalion equipped with T-62s, and 146th Armoured Battalion equipped with T-55s. The other included a battalion of Hezbollah/Lebanon, multiple 'Alawis only' militias controlled by Maher's al-Hossn Association, the IRGC-QF-affiliated Liwa Assad Allah al-Ghallib, and a battalion from the Liwa Nusra az-Zawba'a of the Syrian Socialist National Party (SSNP; a Lebanese-Syrian political party and a para-military organisation with ideology similar to that of the German Nazis of the 1930s and 1940s). Because these units lacked in firepower, they were reinforced by artillery units drawn from the 8th Artillery Regiment, the 120th Artillery Brigade, the 439th Guards Rocket Artillery Brigade, and the 20th Rocket Regiment (the latter equipped with TOS-1A multiple rocket launcher systems, MRLS) of the Russian Army, while four battalion-sized task forces – drawn from the Russian 28th, 32nd, and the 34th Motor Rifle Brigades and the 810th Marines Brigade were securing the secondary lines and supply depots. The purpose of the IV Assault Corps was to attack and destroy the strong concentration of the FSyA units in north-eastern Lattakia (foremost the Turkmen-staffed 1st and 2nd Coastal Divisions), but also the JAN and Ahrar ash-Sham concentrations in the Jishr ash-Shughour area, at the northern tip of the al-Ghab Plain in Western Idlib.

Because of the much more complex situation in northern Hama, organising the diversion for this attack – an assault on the FSyA-held Lataminah salient – proved a far more complex issue. Eventually, it took Maher demonstratively subjecting elements from three 'brigades' of the 4th Division, and another battalion of Hezbollah/Lebanon to the HQ of the 11th Armoured Division in northern Hama, to the command of the Russian advisors, for diverse local militias to agree and join the battle. Armour support was provided by the reconstituted 174th Tank Battalion, while artillery support was provided by several batteries of the Russian Army.

Finally, for an attack on the RTP, the Russian officers advising the HQ of the 10th Armoured Division in Homs had managed to collect a number of BPM-affiliated militias (officially '26th Brigade NDF'), Hezbollah/Syria's Liwa al-Khyber, and at least a battalion of the SSNP's militias.

A T-55 nominally operated by the 'NDF' – though actually by one of SSNP-affiliated militias from northern Hama – as seen in the area south of Kfar Zita, on 7 October 2015. (SSNP release)

SyAAF of 2015

After four years of war, particularly intensive operations in 2012, 2013, and 2014, the loss of several major air bases and more than 100 aircraft and helicopters to combat-related reasons, nearly 400 personnel killed in combat and over 2000 lost to desertions, the SyAAF of 2015 was in tatters. Less than 100 of its aircraft and helicopters were operational at any point in time, and nearly 50 percent of these were at least in need of a major overhaul, if not an outright replacement.[99] Down to about 300 pilots, 2,000 maintenance personnel, and about 1,000 command staff, the strongest component of the air force of the Assad government was meanwhile actually the former air defence branch: integrated into the air force in 2012, it still boasted about 4,000 personnel, many of whom were sons of high military officers or other officials.[100]

Nevertheless, the SyAAF did remain the most effective organized military force under the control of the Assad government. One of the primary reasons was that it was meanwhile largely staffed by

Alawis incited into a frenzy about the supposed Zionist-Wahhabist conspiracy against Syria and the perceived 'extermination of the minorities': in turn, especially unit commanders and their deputies became renowned for boasting about 'burning Sunnis'. The paradox was that those Alawis and the few remaining Sunnis who disbelieved the official propaganda began considering themselves 'trapped' into a relationship of mutual dependency with the government, because they became convinced that the fall of Bashar al-Assad would result in their own downfall, too. Correspondingly, while sometimes (always secretly) blaming the government and the Ba'ath party for dragging them into a war and endangering every one of them, and despite suffering extensive casualties, they remained staunchly loyal to the state and determined to defend the same – through 'defending themselves'. Thus, the SyAAF remained loyal and continued fighting regardless of the chaos around it.

With its units meanwhile referred to as 'Ba'ath Squadrons' (followed by their numerical designation) in most official correspondence, the air force was also more than happy to welcome the Russians, even though these turned down most of the proposals for joint operations and were not willing to provide direct support: the majority of aircraft and helicopters still in service with the SyAAF were long since out of production and then withdrawn from use in Russia, and thus the VKS could not even help with most of the necessary spares. Therefore, these had to be procured by commercial means from Belarus. Similarly, and despite countless rumours, Moscow never delivered any new or even second-hand aircraft to Damascus, and the VKS never attempted to run truly 'joint' operations with the SyAAF: the sole exception from this rule was an attempt related to helicopter operations, described below.[101]

Nevertheless, Moscow did deploy a team of technicians – together with all the necessary equipment and spares – to Sanobar helidrome, where these had gradually overhauled and returned to service about a dozen remaining Kamov Ka-25s and Ka-28s, and Mil Mi-14 helicopters of No. 618 Squadron. Additional spares have been provided for SyAAF fighter-bombers: during the second half of 2015, Su-22s were sighted equipped with drop tanks – for the first time in over a year. Finally, the IRGC-QF organized a transfer of four ex-Iraqi Su-22s from its own fleet

Around 30 Su-22M-2/3s and Su-22M-4s represented the backbone of the SyAAF's fighter-bomber fleet as of October 2015. This Su-22M-4 (serial 3003) was one of about a dozen locally-overhauled examples in service with Shayrat-based No. 677 Squadron. (Pit Weinert Collection)

Table 5: SyAAF Order of Battle, August 2015

Base	Brigade	Squadron	Equipment	Notes
22nd Air Division, HQ Shayrat				
Kweres	77th Training Brigade	-	MFI-15-200A, L-39ZA/ZO	all aircraft non-operational
Sanobar	59th Helicopter Brigade	618 Squadron	Mi-14, Ka-25/28	undergoing overhauls
Dayr az-Zawr	24th Fighter-Bomber Brigade	10 Squadron	MiG-21MF/bis	7-8 aircraft
		17 Squadron	L-39ZA/ZO	4 aircraft
Hama	14th Fighter-Bomber Brigade	678 Squadron	MiG-23MF/MLD	4-6 aircraft
		679 Squadron	MiG-21bis/UM	7-8 aircraft
	63rd Helicopter Brigade	255 Squadron	Mi-8/17	6-7 helicopters
Shayrat	50th Fighter-Bomber Brigade	675 Squadron	MiG-23MF/MLD	14 aircraft
		677 Squadron	Su-22M-4	7-8 aircraft
		685 Squadron	Su-22M-3	6-7 aircraft
	86th Helicopter Brigade	767 Squadron	Mi-25/Mi-35	6 helicopters; mixed Russian-Syrian crews
T.4/Tiyas	70th Fighter-Bomber Brigade	19 Squadron	Su-24MK2	8 aircraft
		827 Squadron	Su-22M-2/3	10 aircraft
20th Air Division, HQ Dmeyr				
Nassiriyah	20th Fighter-Bomber Brigade	698 Squadron	MiG-23BN	7-8 aircraft
as-Seen	17th Fighter-Bomber Brigade	696 Squadron	Su-24MK2	8 aircraft
		697 Squadron	MiG-23BN	6-7 aircraft
		699 Squadron	MiG-29SM/UB	14-16 aircraft
Dmeyr	30th Fighter-Bomber Brigade	67 Squadron	MiG-23MLD	6-7 aircraft
		77 Squadron	MiG-23BN	6-7 aircraft
		947 Squadron	Su-22M-2/3	7-8 aircraft
Almazza	59th Helicopter Brigade	532 Squadron	Mi-8/17	8-9 helicopters
		976 Squadron	SA.342	12-16 helicopters
		977 Squadron	AS.365/Z-9/Mi-8P	4 helicopters
Damascus IAP	29th Transport Brigade	522 Squadron	Yak-40/40K	2 aircraft
		575 Squadron	Falcon 20F/900	2 aircraft
		585 Squadron	Il-76TD	2 aircraft
Marj Ruhayyl/Bley	30th Helicopter Brigade	765 Squadron	Mi-25	8-9 helicopters
	64th Helicopter Brigade	766 Squadron	Mi-25	8-9 helicopters
Khelkhleh	73rd Fighter-Bomber Brigade	54 Squadron	MiG-23MLD/UB	5-6 aircraft
		946 Squadron	MiG-23MF/MLD	4-5 aircraft

to Syria, later the same year. Although theoretically overhauled at Mehrabad before their 'delivery', these turned out to be in such a poor technical condition, that at least three were lost within two weeks of their arrival in Syria. Overall, due to all the related efforts, the SyAAF's sortie rate rose from around 40 per day to nearly 70 per day by the end of 2015.

Days of TOWs

Prepared in a great rush, the offensives run by HQs of the IV Assault Corps, the 10th and 11th Armoured Divisions were launched on the morning of 7 October 2015. The assaults were preceded by massive artillery barrages provided by their organic artillery and by that of the Russian Army units, and a total of 26 combat sorties by fighter-bombers of the VKS, which attacked 11 different targets well behind the battlefield. Because of relatively bad weather over some parts of the battlefield, additional fire-support was provided by four warships of the Russian Caspian Sea Fleet, which launched a total of 26 3M14T Kalibr NK (ASCC-code 'SS-N-27 Sizzler') cruise missiles at another 11 targets – all of these in the Idlib and Aleppo provinces.[102]

The first to start moving were diverse militias subordinated to the 11th Armoured Division, which launched a pincer attack on both sides of the Lataminah Salient. However, while advancing on the village of Kfar Naboudah, seven kilometres north-west of Lataminah, the 174th Tank Battalion was mauled by BGM-71A TOW anti-tank guided missiles operated by the Tajamu al-Azza, 13th Division and Liwa Fursan al-Haq of the FSyA, and the Liwa Suqour al-Ghab (Islamic Front): at least five out of 18-20 MBTs, and 4 BMP-1 infantry fighting vehicles (IFVs) involved were knocked out, while at least one T-72 was captured intact. Furthermore, the attackers lost 33 killed in action, including Lieutenant-General Shafiq al-Fayyad. Concluding their artillery barrages were leaving the insurgents unimpressed, the Russian commanders ordered a new attack west of Lataminah salient on the next morning. Apparently spear-headed by the Hezbollah, the attackers did manage to reach this village and entrench themselves inside.[103] Unknown to almost everybody involved at the time, 8 October 2015 was a particularly important day because of a decision with far-reaching consequences taken in Washington, where the US President Barack Obama issued an order for the US military and intelligence services to cease all support for the FSyA.[104]

As the fighting went on, on 9 October 2015, Ahrar ash-Sham fired a volley of BM-21s at Lattakia and claimed to have shelled

Hmeimim AB with one of its M-54 cannons. While no damage is known to have been caused to the Russian base, at least six civilians were killed on the streets of the biggest Syrian port. The VKS reacted promptly – with attacks by helicopter gunships, and by finding and bombing the HQ of the 13th Division FSyA. Furthermore, the Russians hit the US-supported units deployed on the frontlines opposite to Daesh, in the Infantry School area, north of Aleppo. The extremists promptly exploited the opportunity to launch their attack and collapse the frontlines: over 300 Syrian insurgents were killed or captured and butchered by Daesh, which then went on to blow up one of the electric power plants north of the city: Moscow then cynically put the blame for the destruction of this facility upon the USA.[105]

A warship of the Caspian Sea Fleet launching a 3M14T Kalibr NK cruise missile in direction of Syria, on 7 October 2015. (Russian Ministry of Defence)

One of two Su-25SMs of the VKS that bombed an IDP-camp near Baloun, in Idlib, on 13 October 2015, killing at least six and injuring more than a dozen civilians. (FSyA release)

A Su-34 (Bort '22 Red', RF-95005, see the colour section for details) taking off for a strike sortie from Hmeimim AB, armed with four FAB-500M54s, on 13 October 2015. (Russian Ministry of Defence)

On 10 October, Russian advisors of the 11th Armoured Division took the FSyA in northern Hama by surprise, when they ordered a heliborne assault on the village of Sukayk, east of Lataminah. This was taken after most of the 60th Division FSyA was destroyed, and the Central Division FSyA suffered heavy losses. The VKS, which meanwhile increased the number of Su-24Ms deployed in Syria to 16, reportedly flew 64 combat sorties to hit 55 targets that day – mostly against positions of the Jaysh at-Tawhid (FSyA), inside the RTP, and those of the 1st Coastal Division, in north-eastern Lattakia. Therefore, the insurgents in northern Hama were left free to concentrate and launch a major counterattack in Kfar Naboudah. They overran the Hezbollah battalion entrenched there, killing at least 37 Lebanese combatants, including their commander. With this, the offensive of the reconstituted 11th Armoured Division – which has lost more than 20 armoured vehicles knocked out or captured by the insurgents in one week of combat operations – was de-facto over.[106]

Rout in RTP

Having lost the momentum in northern Hama, the Russian advisors switched their attention to northern Homs, and ordered the militias assigned to the HQ 10th Armoured Division into attacks on the RTP. Despite fierce aerial bombardment and bombastic claims from Moscow, the three-prong attack on the village of el-Ghantu failed to achieve any kind of progress. On the contrary, on 15 October 2015, no less than seven Russian air strikes hit the positions of the BPM and other militias, killing up to 40 combatants including their Syrian commander, Brigadier-General Ma'an Deeb. Although the VKS returned to bomb the RTP even more fiercely the next day, killing between 59 and 65 civilians (including 33 children and 46 people from the same family), this offensive thus ended before it even began.[107] Ignoring fierce critique from the West, and their own failures, the Russians continued pounding the RTP for at least a week longer, killing scores of civilians.

Similar disaster seems to have befallen the first attempt at lifting the siege of the Kweres AB, too: on 11 or 12 October 2015, the forces involved launched an amphibious operation over the Jabbul Lake, hoping to take Daesh by surprise. However, the extremists reacted with a series of typical, fierce counterattacks preceded by suicide vehicle-borne improvised explosive devices (SVBIEDs) that collapsed the ranks of the assailants: for most of the following week the Tiger Force and the IRGC were busy collecting all the troops that fled the battlefield and reorganizing them for the next attempt. Before the involved units were ready for a new attack, on 22 October 2015, Daesh launched another counterattack. Although related reporting remains sketchy, it seems this caused another catastrophe: eventually, it transpired that they were stopped only in the suburbs of as-Safira, principally through an intervention of whatever reinforcements the IRGC-QF was able to throw into the battle.[108]

Overall, early Russian experiences on the battlefields of Syria were not particularly positive. Unrealistic planning by their and inexperienced Iranian officers, poor intelligence and massive underestimation of the Syrian insurgency in particular, poorly selected targets, insufficient artillery and aerial preparation, and the gung-ho tactics of hurriedly-trained forces under their control, had all resulted in minimal gains and heavy losses.

Pilgrimage to Hadher

A similar conclusion is valid for the big offensive the IRGC-QF unleashed through southern Aleppo and into north-eastern Idlib provinces. Even before this operation was launched, the Iranians lost their top commander in Syria, when Major-General Hossein Hamedani was killed in the outskirts of Aleppo, on 8 October 2015, under unclear circumstances.[109] Nevertheless, preparations went on – foremost in the form of an outright 'air bridge' between Iran and Syria, the purpose of which was to deploy dozens of thousands of combatants from the various Iraqi Shi'a militias with the help of Airbus A300B4s of the IRGC-controlled Mahan Air, Airbus A320s of the Syrian Air, Cham Air, and Queshm Air, Boeing 747-131s of Iran Air, and Il-76Ts of the Syrian Air Force, and Lockheed C-130 Hercules transports of the Islamic Republic of Iran Air Force. At the high point of this operation, during the week between 16 and 23 October 2015, no less than 38 such flights were registered. The ultimate result was that the number of independently verified formations of this kind rose from around a dozen in September 2015, to around 60 by February 2016.[110]

Nominally, all the militias in question were established to 'fight the Daesh' (in Iraq), but the motivation of their combatants was extremely diverse and ranging from 'protection of the Shrine of Sayyida Zaynab' (in southern Damascus), via 'my Imam told me to go', to 'want to slaughter Ba'athists'. Wearing designations with indisputably religious backgrounds, most of the groups were put through short training courses at diverse camps in Iran, and then flown to Damascus and Aleppo. Because the IRGC-QF wanted to lift the siege of Shi'a populated enclaves north-west of Aleppo and north of Idlib, the majority of these were concentrated in the Aleppo area. The best equipped and largest amongst them were the Kata'ib Hezbollah (de-facto Hezbollah/Iraq) and the Harakat an-Nujba. Moreover, the IRGC-QF had expanded the North Aleppo-based Palestinian militia Liwa al-Qods al-Filistini to about 4,000 combatants, while its original brigade staffed by Afghan Hazaras – Liwa Fatemiyoun – was expanded into a division consisting of four brigades. Finally, while successfully spoiling an attempt of the regular Iranian army to place an order for 300 T-90 main battle tanks (MBTs) in Russia, the IRGC-QF acquired 24 such vehicles for its own purposes: notably, six each of these were distributed between the Tiger Force, the Liwa Suqour as-Sahra (a PMC run by Jaber brothers), Kata'ib Hezbollah and Harakat an-Nujba. Similarly, nearly all of the remaining T-72 of the former SAA, and a batch of about 20 T-72AVs acquired from Russia in October 2015, were taken up by the Liwa Fatemiyoun and assorted Iraqi Shi'a militias. These units were supported by a battalion-sized task force including troops from the 7th Guards Assault Division, the 27th Guards Motor Rifle Brigade, and several artillery batteries of the Russian Army.

Also deployed in the area south of Aleppo was a colourful group of units the task of which was to lift the Daesh's siege of the Kweres AB. Sometimes reported as the 2nd Division, this was led by the Tiger Force and included several battalions of the BPM, the Liwa Imam al-Bakr – which came into being through the combination of diverse Hezbollah/Syria formations from the Aleppo area – and IRGC-QF's Liwa Zainebiyoun, staffed by the Pakistani Shi'a. Fire-support was provided by elements of the 61st Marine Brigade and a battalion of the 74th Guards Motor Rifle Brigade of the Russian Army. In this fashion, the Russians – but especially the IRGC-QF – managed to tilt the balance of forces in northern and north-western Syria significantly in favour of the 'pro-Assad' camp.

The IRGC-QF-run offensive into southern Aleppo was initiated on the morning of 15 October 2015. Although the IRGC is often famed as an 'elite' force by different military observers in the West, this was anything other than a classic infiltration attack as undertaken so often by its formations during the Iran-Iraq War of the 1980s: instead, the Iranian officers deployed their artillery and tanks to pound enemy positions – primarily held by the JAN – until these ceased firing back, and then launched frontal infantry attacks. The result was a grim battle of attrition that lasted for nearly a month, forced over 50,000 civilians to flee in the direction of Turkey, and ended with the JAN losing the town of Hadher and being driven all the way back to the M5 highway – though in exchange for extensive losses of IRGC-QF-controlled formations. Indeed, the frontlines began to stabilise only with the arrival of the TOW-equipped Liwa Sultan Murad (FSyA) in the Khan Touman area, which hit the right flank of the Iranian advance, knocking out about a dozen MBTs and other vehicles, on 19 and 20 October 2015. The VKS became involved in battles in this part of Syria starting with 23 October, when it bombed villages behind the battlefield. However, not only due to the lack of differential GLONASS stations in this part of Syria, but also because of poor coordination with the IRGC-QF, its bombs had no effect upon

Although meanwile replaced as CO IRGC-QF in Syria by Major-General Mohammad Jafar Assadi (aka 'Abu Ahmad'), Qassem Soleimani remained a figurehead, and frequently toured the battlefields to bolster the morale of the troops. This photograph shows him while speaking to a group of IRGC-QF-troops in the Aleppo area on 13 October 2015. (IRGC-QF release)

the insurgents and the JAN. Furthermore, the latter repeatedly raided the crucial road connecting Hama and Homs with Ithriya, and then with Khan Nassir – the sole land connection between Damascus and Aleppo remaining – thus interrupting the flow of supplies. After losing Reza Khavari, the commander of the Liwa Fatemiyoun in this area, the IRGC-QF was forced to secure this road by establishing dozens of checkpoints controlled by the Liwa al-Qods al-Filistini and other militias. Even then, this was only an overture to the final battle for Aleppo, which was to culminate 12 months later.

A group of combatants from the Liwa al-Qods – a unit staffed by children of Palestinian refugees primarily from the Hindarat Camp, north of Aleppo. (IRGC release)

A platoon of T-72s operated by IRGC-QF's Kata'ib Hezbollah, in southern Aleppo province, on 1 November 2015. (al-Mannar)

A combatant from IRGC-QF's Harakat an-Nujba atop an (IRGC-owned) T-90 in southern Aleppo province, in late October 2015. (al-Mannar)

War on the Turkmen

Meanwhile, the situation in north-eastern Lattakia was heating up. Within a fortnight of their deployment to Syria, VKS Su-24s and Su-30SMs violated Turkish airspace at least three times: once on 3, once on 4, and once on 6 October 2015. Moreover, one of the Su-30SMs had locked-on its radar on a Lockheed F-16C Fighting Falcon interceptor of the Turkish Air Force (Türk Havva Kuvvetleri, THK), underway north of the border, for a full 5

minutes and 40 seconds. In another case, on 6 October, a Su-30SM had locked on a THK F-16C for 4 minutes and 30 seconds.[111]

In modern military flying, such behaviour is considered not only reckless, but outright an aggressive action. Unsurprisingly, Ankara reacted with fierce protests, even more so when a Russian mini-UAV was either shot down or crashed on its territory, on 10 October 2015. With relations between the USA and Turkey still being relatively good at the time, the US Air Force reacted by flying its Lockheed-Martin F-22 Raptor 'stealth' fighters over Syria: following one encounter between these and at least one of the Su-30SMs on the same day, the Russians suddenly ceased with their provocations. Indeed, Moscow subsequently issued something similar to an apology, explaining violations of the Turkish airspace with navigational mistakes. Furthermore, in an attempt to lessen tensions, the Deputy Commander VKS, Major-General Sergey Dronov, visited Ankara to meet representatives of the Turkish government and the THK on 15 October 2015. Amongst other points, he reached an agreement to make use of not only the international 'guard' frequency (121.5KHz) but also an additional, 'special' frequency (243MHz) as a direct link of communication between the THK and the VKS. Furthermore, Dronov agreed to announce any kind of VKS operations in the proximity of the Turkish border at least 12 hours in advance.[112]

In return, Ankara reiterated its warning that it would shoot down any military aircraft violating its airspace: this was repeated – via the media and on diplomatic channels – no less than 35 times over the following 30 days, while the THK intensified its combat air patrols (CAPs) along the border (flown continuously since the outbreak of violence in Syria). Apparently unimpressed, the VKS meanwhile directed an increasing number of air strikes against positions of the 1st Costal Division FSyA, and villages predominantly populated by the Turkmen minority, in northern Lattakia – in what was clearly a breach of Article 51 of Protocol I to the Geneva Convention regarding attacks on civilians. As a wave of over 60,000 refugees fled over the border to Turkey, Ankara not only protested against attacks on its minority living in Syria since the 11th Century, but also demanded a meeting of the UN Security Council (UNSC). However, its requests were ignored by the international community, while Moscow cynically explained its air strikes and artillery barrages as 'bombing militants of the IS'.[113]

That Moscow was unimpressed by Turkish protests was obvious already by 15 October 2015, when the IV Assault Corps launched its offensive on Salma, once a holiday resort dominating the mountains of northern Lattakia. Despite hard pushing by Russian advisers and from Damascus, after four days of fierce artillery barrages and repeated assaults, the involved units only captured two peaks and three minor villages. The fiercest battles were fought for the village of Ghammam, controlled by the 1st Coastal Division FSyA, the commander of which, Basil Zamo, proved a skilled and imaginative tactician. Indeed, on 18 October, one of his mortar teams hit one of the enemy forward observation posts at Jebel Nabi Yunis, reportedly killing numerous officers – including three Russians. In return, Zamo was killed in one of the Russian air strikes that hit the villages of Bsafirah and Meshirfih on 20 October, but his unit continued fighting, regardless the odds. The advance on Salma thus failed to gain any momentum even once the attackers secured Katf al-Ghadar, a hill overlooking this town, on 23 October: on the contrary, Ghammam changed hands at least four times before it was finally secured by – according to insurgents – an attack of the Russian Army, on 10 November 2015.[114]

Overall, during the first month of the Russian military intervention in Syria, the 32 combat aircraft of the VKS originally known to be present in the country, had officially flown 1,292 combat sorties against 1,623 targets. Setting a pattern for the future, the MOD in Moscow declared every single air strike 'successful', every single bomb a 'direct hit', and every single target as 'destroyed'.[115]

A Mi-24P of the VKS releasing decoy flares near a target in the Sukayk area on 10 October 2015. (Syrian social media)

A Su-30SM rolling down the runway of Hmeimim AB on 1 October 2015. (Russian MOD)

A still from a video showing a Mi-24P during an attack on the RTP in November 2015. (FSyA release)

A Su-34 (Bort '21 Red') taking-off from Hmeimim AB for a strike sortie in November 2015. (Russian Ministry of Defence)

Restrained Helicopter Operations

The Russian military has traditionally put heavy emphasis on the use of attack helicopters for providing CAS to its ground troops, and on the use of heliborne troops in special purpose roles. Correspondingly, the VKS did deploy a strong helicopter component to Syria. However, operations of its Mi-24s in October 2015 can only be described as 'restrained'. Supported by FACs, these went into action over the battlefield in northern Hama on 8 and 9 October 2015, with the aim of attacking enemy troop concentrations and strong points. Knowing that helicopters are ill-suited for urban combat, and because of poor targeting intelligence, the Russians sought to deploy them only against open-country targets. Furthermore, they attempted to combine

their Mi-24s with Mi-25s of the SyAAF, where one of the Russian helicopters would lead one of the Syrian. Early experiences were not particularly positive. Not only were several Russian helicopters damaged, but the SyAAF Mi-25 flown by Lieutenant Khalid Wardy was shot down by ground fire near Kfar Naboudah on 9 October 2015.

Finding themselves exposed to all sorts of ground fire, and lacking targets for their guided missiles, the Russians reacted by flying higher and operating either from outside, or from the limit of the envelope of numerous heavy machine guns used by the insurgents and the JAN, from where they would fire their unguided 80mm rockets 'spray and pray' fashion. Such tactics not only significantly degraded the effectiveness of their attacks, but also failed to keep them safe: after several helicopters suffered light damage from ground fire, a VKS Mi-24 was damaged severely over the RTP, and forced to make an emergency landing behind friendly positions on 24 October 2015. Subsequently, Russian helicopters rarely flew over insurgent and/or JAN-positions in north-western Syria. Instead, by early 2016, the VKS donated six of its old Mi-24s to the SyAAF, and for a while ran a joint unit staffed by its own and SyAAF crews, based at Shayrat.

Show-Campaign against IS

On 31 October 2015, an Airbus A321-231 operated by the Russian airline Kogalymavia (colloquially known as 'Metrojet') underway on Flight 9268, from Sharm el-Sheikh in Egypt to Pulkovo IAP, near Saint Petersburg, in Russia, crashed into the desert of the northern Sinai, killing all 224 on board. Shortly after this tragedy, Daesh's 'Sinai Branch' claimed responsibility for destruction of this aircraft. This thesis was quickly adopted by multiple Egyptian and Russian officials, irrespective of the results of the subsequent investigation. Correspondingly, the MOD in Moscow demonstratively ordered the VKS into attacks on Daesh, especially its 'capital', the city of Raqqa: on 3 November 2015, Su-34s from Hmeimim AB flew up to 20 strikes, deploying – amongst others – KAB-1500 LGBs. Two days later, Su-34s bombed the market in al-Bukamal, in southern Dayr az-Zawr province, killing 71 civilians and injuring more than 100. However, because most of the VKS aircraft at Hmeimim AB had an effective combat range of only 250-300 kilometres, most of the Daesh-controlled areas were outside their reach. Furthermore, the 40 Sukhois meanwhile present at Hmeimim AB began showing first signs of wear: according to US defence officials, nearly a third were grounded due to the impact of the weather and elements, but also the general inexperience in expeditionary operations. Thus, it took the Russians more than a week to prepare anything like an 'all-out' effort to hit Daesh. Amongst others, at least four Su-25SMs and between four and six Mi-24 helicopters had to be forward deployed at T.4 AB for this purpose. Even then, when 'Operation Retaliation' was launched, on 17 November 2015, it had to receive support from bomber-units based in Russia.[116]

Starting at 0500hrs that morning, 12 Tupolev Tu-22M-3 bombers from Mozdok AB (in the Republic of North Ossetia) flew their first round of air strikes on the Daesh-controlled parts of northern and eastern Syria, each armed with 12 250 kilogram bombs, or 6 500 kilogram bombs. Later the same day, two Tupolev Tu-160 strategic bombers fired a total of 16 Kh-101 cruise missiles while underway over the eastern Mediterranean Sea, while three Tupolev Tu-95MS-1 and Tu-95MS-8 strategic bombers fired an unknown number of Kh-555 cruise missiles while underway over northern Iran. On the last day of this operation, 20 November 2015, eight Su-34s from Krymsk AB on the Russian-occupied Crimean Peninsula flew a total of 16 combat sorties over Syria, too. In this fashion, the VKS had managed to accumulate a total of 143 combat sorties on one day (20 November 2015), or 522 in four days. Tu-95MS and Tu-160s flew 16 of these (all from Engels AB, near Saratov), releasing a total of 85 cruise missiles, including 48 Kh-101 and 16 Kh-555s by Tu-160s, and 19 Kh-555s by Tu-95s – mostly from within Iranian airspace (warships and submarines of the Russian Navy added 18 additional cruise missiles). About 20 Tu-22M-3s meanwhile gathered at Mozdok, launched no less than 96 sorties to release 1,400 tonnes of bombs. The MOD in Moscow claimed that these air strikes alone had 'destroyed' no less than 826 targets.[117]

Characterising this 'Retaliation Campaign' as a 'military operation' is rather problematic: the successful lifting of the siege of Kweres AB, on 10 November 2015 (by a mix of units controlled by the Tiger Force and the IRGC-QF), took place before the Russian aerial onslaught was even launched, and not one of the VKS air strikes is known to have provided direct support for this operation. On the contrary, the majority of Russian air strikes flown between 17 and 20 November did not hit Daesh, but the Syrian opposition and civilians living in the areas controlled by the same, and their effectiveness was highly questionable. Not only that four of the missiles released by VKS Tu-95s are known

to have failed on launch, or shortly after, and crashed inside Iran: many of those that had reached Syria then failed too. For example, out of six missiles that approached the area of Kansafra, in western Aleppo, four failed shortly before reaching the (presumed) targets, one disappeared without a trace, and one demolished the local school (fortunately, this was empty). What kind of damage was caused in places like Darat Izza, Urum al-Kubra and Hayyan remains unknown, and the same is valid for missiles that targeted diverse points around Ma'arat an-Nauman and Abu ad-Duhor. In Idlib (city), one missile is known to have demolished the local conserve factory, while another detonated right above one of the major streets, causing dozens of civilian casualties. At least two Russian cruise missiles reportedly hit friendly positions: one fell within the area of the so-called 'Defence Laboratories' (ammunition factories), in IRGC-QF-controlled as-Safira, while another hit a local SAA HQ in western Aleppo, reportedly causing up to 36 casualties.[118]

Furthermore, once released, sub-sonic cruise missiles needed up to two hours to reach their targets and could not be re-directed. This meant that they could only hit fixed targets. This was of particular importance for strikes that should have targeted Daesh: as of autumn 2015, the extremists in northern and eastern Syria were operating in small, mobile detachments, which proved hard to find and track even for much better-equipped Western militaries. Certainly enough, Daesh had numerous offices in the Raqqa area and was in control of nearly all of the oil and gas-industry in the Dayr az-Zawr area, but most of these were operated by local civilians – which Daesh generally considered non-trustworthy, if

Escorted by a Su-30SM, this Tu-160 was photographed while releasing a Kh-555 cruise missile against targets in Syria on 20 November 2015.

A pair of Tu-22M-3s each unleashing a string of 12 OFAB-250-270 bombs over north-eastern Syria on 20 November 2015. (Russian Ministry of Defence)

A Su-30SM escorting one of two Tu-160 bombers over Syria on 20 November 2015. (Russian Ministry of Defence)

not '2nd class citizens'. While some of VKS' air strikes did hit such facilities their effects were also hard to quantify, because during the same period of time, the Central Command of the US military (CENTCOM) ran its Operation Tidal Wave II, in the course of which it systematically destroyed most of the system for crude extraction and transportation used by Daesh to place resulting products on the domestic and international black market. Finally, a cross-examination of videos released by the MOD in Moscow had once again shown a large degree of mis-identified targets. One of the most reliably confirmed targeting errors included a video showing what was declared as an 'attack on militant tent camp': bombed by at least one Tu-22M-3: this turned out to be a granary, with stacks of grain sacks covered by sailcloth. Similarly, what the MOD proudly declared an 'oil refinery…destroyed by guided missiles', turned out to be a water treatment plant near Aleppo.[119]

Fateful 24 November

On the morning of 24 November, around 0942hrs local time, early warning radars of the THK detected the take-off of two unknown aircraft from Hmeimim AB. Widely separated, these climbed to an altitude of 5,791m (19,000ft) and entered an orbit above the town of Jishr ash-Shughour: one circling south of the southern-most tip of the Turkish border, the other nearly 10 kilometres further east. Because – contrary to agreements between Ankara and Moscow from 15 October – the Russians did not announce this mission close to the Turkish border, the THK was thus unaware of the nationality of the two aircraft. As these went into action, and approached the border, and then flew an orbit parallel to it, over the following five minutes the THK issued 10 radio warnings on both of the agreed frequencies, demanding them to divert south.

When the Russians failed to react, and then took a course in the direction of Turkish airspace, a pair of F-16Cs airborne on a CAP station over the northern Hatay was issued clearance to open fire. Therefore, as the two unknown aircraft approached Turkey, the F-16s went into action. The first unknown aircraft had briefly crossed Turkish airspace before turning south, but did so before THK's interceptors were in a position to open fire. The eastern unknown aircraft followed in fashion: shortly

before it entered the Turkish airspace, the lead F-16 fired one AIM-120C missile from beyond visual range. Relative to the Turkish F-16s, the two unknown aircraft were up-sun, between 15 and 20 kilometres away and thus 'invisible' (THK's ROEs for such cases did not require a visual identification). Thus, the firing of the AIM-120 was, de-facto, a snap-shot, taken under difficult circumstances as the target was moving perpendicular to the F-16s: most pulse-Doppler radars – including the APG-68s installed on THK's F-16Cs – have a problem with tracking targets under such circumstances because of the well-known issue with the so-called 'Doppler shift'. Nevertheless, the

Reportedly, the Su-24M '83 White' was the aircraft shot down by a Turkish F-16C on 24 November 2015. (Russian Ministry of Defence)

Captain Konstantin Muratkin, the bombardier/navigator of the downed Sukhoi, was recovered from the insurgent-controlled area in a combined operation of Russian and Hezbollah special forces (the latter are recognizable on this photograph by their black uniforms). (Syrian Ministry of Defence)

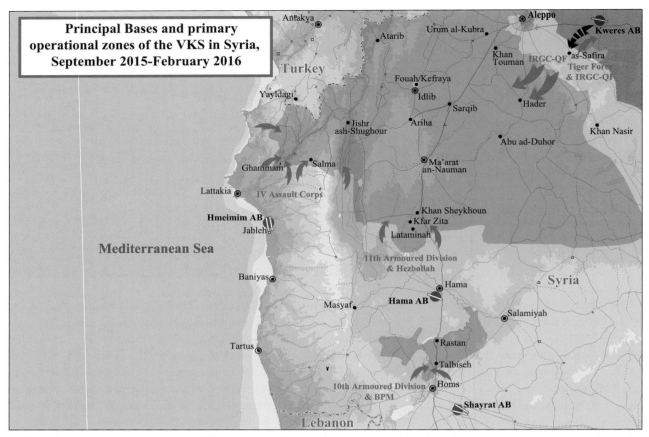

Map 1 The primary operational zone of the VKS (and most of the Russian ground forces) – all of which was in north-western Syria – during the first six months of the intervention, dispositions of the IV Assault Corps, the IRGC-QF's force in southern Aleppo, and principal directions of their ground offensives. The shaded areas were controlled by Syrian insurgents and the HTS in the Idlib province and north-eastern Lattakia, as well as native insurgents in northern Homs and southern Hama: at the start of the intervention, FSyA positions in Ghammam were only some 35 kilometres away from Hmeimim AB. The Daesh-controlled areas (right upper corner of the map) were on the verge of effective combat range of most of the Russian aircraft and helicopters based at Hmeimim AB, and thus attacked either by Su-34s, or by bombers based in Russia. (Map by Tom Cooper)

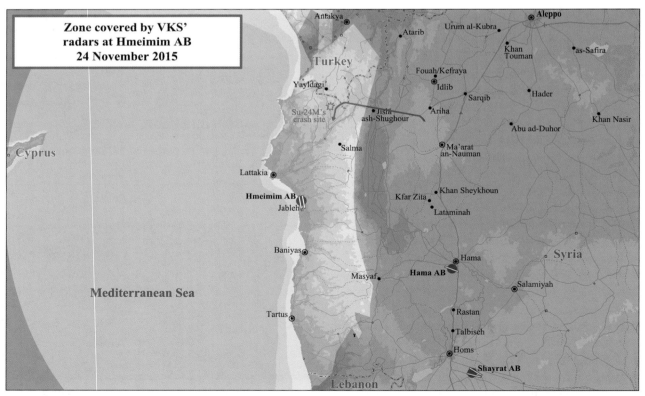

Map 2 The same area illustrating how limited the Russian radar coverage was over north-western Syria as of 24 November 2015. Although the radars positioned at Hmeimim AB could – theoretically – detect high-flying aircraft the size of an airliner over 300 kilometres away, their coverage of altitudes below 6,000 metres (roughly 18,000ft) was blocked by the local geography – foremost the Jebel an-Nusayriayah mountains in the east, but also by mountains in the Hatay province of Turkey. The arrow in the upper centre denotes the approximate course flown by Russian Su-24s before one of them was shot down on 24 November 2015. (Map by Tom Cooper)

missile proximity fused closely underneath its target, spraying its fuselage and wing with shrapnel.

Streaming burning fuel, what transpired to be a Sukhoi Su-24M2 'Bort 83' of the VKS flipped out of control and plunged towards the ground. The aircraft crashed into the hills about two kilometres south of the Turkish border, approximately at GPS-coordinates 35° 51' 37.64" N, 36° 00' 17.98" E. The crew, consisting of Lieutenant-Colonel Oleg Peshkov and Captain Konstantin Muratkin, ejected but were almost immediately taken under fire by a group of jihadists that were Turkish citizens and members of the Turkish ultra-nationalist organisation 'Grey Wolves', which sided with the al-Qaeda-linked Jabhat an-Nusra. It is generally assessed that these killed Peshkov with machine-gun fire while he was still under the parachute: an act that, if ever confirmed, would constitute a war crime.

Obviously uncertain about how to react, the Russians at Hmeimim AB were slow in launching a combat search and rescue (CSAR) operation. This was initiated only three hours later, when the VKS deployed two pairs of helicopters to search for the downed crew: each comprised one Mi-8ATMSh-V CSAR-helicopter, escorted by a single Mi-24. In the course of this operation, the Mi-8 Bort 252 was hit by ground fire and forced to make an emergency landing at GPS-coordinates 35° 40' 54.10" N, 36° 4' 47.50" E. One of 12 crewmembers and Russian Marines on board, Private Aleksander Pazynich, was shot in the neck and killed. Shortly after the helicopter was evacuated, it was destroyed by a TOW ATGM of the 1st Coastal Division FSyA. The crew of the downed helicopter, and Captain Muratkin were subsequently extracted with the help of a team of 12 Syrian and 6 Hezbollah special forces operators.[120]

CHAPTER 4
MARCH ON ALEPPO

The downing of the VKS Su-24M on 24 November 2015 not only put Russia and Turkey – and thus NATO – on the verge of an armed conflict, but prompted Moscow into an all-out propaganda offensive. The Turkish decision to open fire at aircraft that violated the Turkish airspace for 'only about two kilometres' and a duration of 'only 17 seconds' was declared an 'aggressive overreaction', while Putin declared it a 'stab in the back'. Turkish attempts to contact the crew before opening fire were all denied, and a fake story about F-16s violating Syrian airspace to down the Su-24 with the help of AIM-9 Sidewinder short-range missiles launched instead: ironically, this proved so ill-devised, that the Kremlin and the Ministry of Defence in Moscow were forced to correct it several times. Moreover, Moscow imposed damaging economic sanctions against Ankara, and then opened a campaign of isolating the Turkish government on the international stage. Ably supported not only by the ill-advised actions of the government of the Turkish President Recep Tayyip Erdogan, but also diverse of his opponents in the EU and NATO, this plot proved highly successful – it also managed to divert at least a part of the public attention away from what the Russians were meanwhile doing in Syria.

Patching Holes

The direct, military-related consequences of the downing of the Russian Su-24 by Turkish F-16s were actually limited – and principally related to the fact that many of the adored high-tech weapons supposedly used by the VKS in Syria have either never entered production, or were at least never purchased by the GenStab, but only sold to export customers. The best example of this was the lack of R-77 (ASCC-code 'AA-12 Adder') active radar homing air-to-air missiles. Although famed in public for decades, and widely exported, these were never acquired by the VKS: the MOD lacked the money to buy any, and the loss of control over Ukraine forced it to order their production in Russia, starting in 2016. Thus, until late November 2015, even the famed Su-30SMs and Su-34s deployed at Hmeimim AB were still armed with obsolete R-27R/T (ASCC-code 'AA-10 Alamo') and R-73 (ASCC-code 'AA-11 Archer') air-to-air missiles. While a batch of R-77 was eventually acquired from an unknown source (possibly from SyAAF's stocks), the air defences of Hmeimim AB thus had to be bolstered through the addition of the cutting-edge S-400 SAM-system (ASCC-code 'SA-21 Growler'), deployed with help of An-124 transports, on 26 November 2015.[121]

Much more important proved the decision to deploy at least four Su-34s to Hmeimim AB, by 6 December, followed by four Su-24s, and then at least four Mi-35M attack helicopters, later the same month. Finally, in January 2016, the VKS sent four of its brand-new Sukhoi Su-35S multi-role fighters to Syria. From the point of view of Moscow, but also its military commanders in Syria, additional airframes were urgently necessary. While there is no doubt that the 'fire-power demonstrations' of October and November 2015, and associated propaganda campaigns have left lasting impressions upon numerous Western observers and reluctant politicians, the hard reality was that it fell short of desired effects. Therefore, the decision was reached to not only 'avenge' the loss of the Su-24, but outright 'punish' Turkey – widely, through wrongly, declared as being the primary supporter of extremist Islamic terrorism in Syria – by expanding and intensifying the bombardment of civilians in parts of Syria controlled by the insurgency. While the air strikes by the SyAAF and the VKS hit 'only' four hospitals by 20 October 2015, and such attacks could be described as an 'exception', subsequently they became a norm. Similarly, the VKS began making the widespread use of CBUs – especially for attacks on urban centres. When this caused an international outburst, Moscow reacted cynically, though also in a fashion bordering on tragicomedy: the use of CBUs was flatly denied by the MOD even while Kremlin-controlled media repeatedly published videos of Su-34s armed with different variants of the well-known RBK-500 series of CBUs. They then ceased releasing its official number of daily air strikes and nearly ceased publishing targeting videos too, on 20 and 24 November 2015, respectively.[122]

'03 Red', one from the second batch of Su-34s deployed by the VKS in Syria starting in November 2015, loaded with a total of six FAB-500M-62 general purpose bombs, a pair of R-73s, and a pair of KAB-500S-Es – probably the heftiest load observed in three years of the Russian intervention. (Russian Ministry of Defence)

Aerial Onslaught – on Civilians

Meanwhile, and for all the reasons listed above, the VKS joined the SyAAF in systematically targeting civilians and the civilian infrastructure of north-western Syria. Facilities like water plants, wells, marketplaces, bakeries, food depots, and even aid convoys underway from Turkey in the direction of Aleppo were subjected to repeated and intentional air strikes with an obvious aim: punishing and driving civilians out of insurgent-controlled areas. In 5,240 combat sorties officially announced by the MOD in Moscow, as flown by the VKS in Syria between 30 September and 31 December 2015, no less than 330 incidents in which civilians were killed have been registered. At least 192 of these were reliably

concluded as involving VKS aircraft, in which at least 1,098, more likely between 1,826 and 2,426 civilian, non-combat deaths were caused. Although taken aback by media attention and detailed reporting in this regard, Moscow flatly denied all of the related allegations, and insisted on not having killed a single Syrian civilian: at the same time the VKS even reinforced its assaults on the civilian population, dedicating most of about 6,500 sorties flown in the period between 24 December 2015 and 22 February 2016 (an average 107 a day) to related targets.[123] It was only months later that the cumulative effects of this campaign – including its consequences for the fighting on the ground, but also for the political situation in general – were to become obvious.

A convoy of civilian trucks carrying aid provided by one of the Turkish NGOs for civilians in eastern Aleppo, burning following Russian air strikes on the roads in the Azaz area, in northern Syria, on 28 November 2015. (via R. S.)

The Su-25SM '25 Red' rolling back to its parking spot after a combat sortie over the Idlib province, in November 2015. (Russian Ministry of Defence)

By November 2015, some of the Su-24Ms at Hmeimim AB were re-serialled, as obvious on this example (registration RF-90943), which arrived in Syria wearing the bort '04 White' (note traces on its fin). This photograph shows it carrying four FAB-500M-62 general purpose bombs. (Russian Ministry of Defence)

This photograph from 11 November 2015, shows a Su-24Ms in rarely seen configuration: carrying four BETAB-500 concrete-piercing bombs, designed to destroy reinforced concrete shelters, runways, dams, ship locks, railway bridges and warships. In Syria, the VKS deployed BETAB-500s not only to target underground facilities used by insurgents, but also multi-storey apartment buildings in cities like Idlib and Aleppo. (Russian Ministry of Defence)

Fatal Blows

After three months of sustained bombardment, artillery barrages and ground attacks on the 1st and 2nd Coastal Divisions in northern Lattakia, in mid-December 2015 the Russian advisers to the HQ IV Assault Corps concluded that it was the time to effect a major break-through. Correspondingly, they organized reinforcements in the form of an entire 'brigade' of Hezbollah/Lebanon, and the Liwa Suqour as-Sahra PMC. The result was an onslaught that the massively weakened 1st Coastal Division could not stand any more: starting with 16 December, it began withdrawing from Jebel an-Nuba and other hilltops, and from 10 different villages. Reinforcements rushed in by the JAN proved insufficient: the crucial town of Salma was surrounded from three sides and, following additional bombardment and ground attacks, secured by the Axis by the evening of 12 January 2016. In the course of the next week, the IV Assault Corps pushed up the Jebel al-Akrad and the Turkmen Mountain, and eventually seized Rabia, on 20 January. The VKS provided sustained CAS and interdiction strikes for this operation, reportedly flying no less than 522 related sorties between 12 and 25 January 2016. Realizing that the 1st Coastal Division FSyA had suffered up to 50 percent losses, the Russians continued pressing their allies: by the morning of 18 February, Axis forces then captured even the town of Kinsabba, thus finally pushing the insurgents outside the artillery range to Lattakia and Qardaha (the heartland of the Assad clan).[124]

However, and rather ironically, the biggest blow against the insurgency in this period – and then one of three blows that was to prove decisive for the subsequent flow of the war in Syria – was instrumented not by the Russians, but by the IRGC-QF, and the part of the Kurdish PKK/PYD/YPG/YPJ-conglomerate that was in control of the so-called Afrin enclave, in north-western Syria.[125]

Keen to lift the siege of Nubol and Zahra, the Iranian officers requested that the Russians bomb the insurgent-controlled corridor between the Turkish border and northern Aleppo, in early February 2016. For once, Moscow reacted positively, and thus the VKS was ordered to subject this area – the so-called Azaz-corridor – to up to 100 air strikes a day, which systematically demolished the insurgent defence positions and blocked the movement of their reinforcements and supplies. By the time the IRGC-QF assaulted, the shaken defenders offered only minimal resistance. Exploiting the pre-occupation of the insurgents with the situation further south, on 10 February 2016 the YPG-units from Afrin then assaulted and captured the Mennagh AB and the nearby town, further north. In this fashion, the crucial corridor connecting the Turkish border with Aleppo was cut off once and for all: this was a blow from which the Syrian insurgency has never recovered.[126]

A column of smoke caused by an air strike rising from the ruins of Salma, as seen from the southern side of that town, in December 2015. (Syrian social media)

A Su-24M loaded with four FAB-500M-54s rolling for take-off from Hmeimim AB on 6 November 2015. This type flew nearly 40 percent of all the sorties of the VKS in Syria during November and December that year. (Russian Ministry of Defence)

Operating almost on the verge of their combat range, Su-25SMs played a crucial role in the intensive campaign against insurgent forces in the so-called Azaz corridor, north of Aleppo, in turn paving the way for the advance of Axis ground forces. Notable on this photograph is the installation of two rarely-seen B-13 pods for five 130mm unguided rockets. (Russian Ministry of Defence)

'Withdrawal' – Russian Style

Following the success north of Aleppo, the Putin government rushed to declare a victory – and present itself as a peacekeeper and a mediator. Although one of the VKS' Tu-214R prototypes deployed at Hmeimim AB around this time was airborne for hours over the Aleppo area every single day during the mid-February 2016 – the GRF in Syria completely failed to detect Daesh's preparations for another raid on Khan Nasir. Certainly enough, the intelligence services of the Assad government and the IRGC-QF failed in this regard, too. Thus, when the extremist attack hit home, during the night from 22 to 23 February 2016, it took everybody by surprise, and resulted in Daesh mauling numerous Iraqi Shi'a and loyalist militias and taking Khan Nassir. Once again, the only supply route for all the Axis forces, and all the Russian troops deployed in the Aleppo area, too – was severed. Certainly enough, the situation was saved by another counterattack of the Hezbollah/

Often described as 'government forces', or at least those of the 4th Armoured Division, the troops that lifted the siege of Nubol and Zahra, and thus cut off the insurgent-controlled corridor between the Turkish border and Aleppo, were from IRGC-QF's units, like the Afghan-Hazara-staffed Liwa Fatemiyoun, visible on this photograph taken in Nubol on 4 February 2016. (al-Mannar release)

Flags wrapping bodies of Axis combatants killed during the fighting north of Aleppo in February 2016 have left little doubt about their nationalities and origins. (al-Mannar release)

Lebanon and the IRGC-QF's Liwa Fatemiyoun, both of which paid a dear price while fighting Daesh's commandos and clearing hundreds of IEDs. The crucial road connecting Khan Nassir with Ithriya – meanwhile littered with burned out hulks of hundreds of fighting-vehicles and other types – was re-opened on 27 or 28 February 2016.[127]

From the standpoint of the Putin government and the Russian armed forces, this never happened. In pursuit of its policy of imposing its conditions upon the armed Syrian opposition, the GRF established the 'Centre for the Reconciliation of the Warring Parties' at Hmeimim AB, on 24 February 2016, and opened negotiations with the USA, Turkey and other involved foreign powers, aiming to conclude the war. The result of this effort was an armistice announced for the evening of 26 February 2016. While the USA and its allies – foremost Turkey, Qatar, and Saudi Arabia – managed to impose a cease-fire upon the insurgency through withdrawing their support, the status of Salafist groups (like Ahrar ash-Sham), but especially that of the JAN (the majority of which traditionally consisted of transnational jihadists), remained unclear. Correspondingly, Moscow excluded them from the cease-fire and, after grounding the VKS for exactly one day, on 27 February 2016, continued the aerial bombardment. Similarly, the IRGC-QF, which always insisted on 'liberating every inch of Syria' – and thus the Assad government, too – never respected the cease-fire. Indeed, as the subsequent developments were to show, the entire affair of 26 February 2016 was a big scam, in best traditions of, 'you cease, the Russians & allies fire' practices well known from the war in Ukraine.[128]

Of course, with the Putin government remaining curious to effect an official end of its adventure in Syria, it went a step further and announced a 'withdrawal' of the Russian forces, on 14 March 2016. Correspondingly, during the following days all 12 Su-25SMs, four Su-24Ms, and at least four Su-34 were flown back to Russia: 'only' 4 Su-35S', 4 Su-34s, 4 Su-30SMs, and 12 Su-24Ms were left behind at Hmeimim AB. On the other hand, the VKS' helicopter regiment was significantly increased through the addition of four Mi-28Ns and four Ka-52 attack helicopters.[129]

First Liberation of Palmyra

Indeed, obviously counting on all of the public in Russia and abroad having the memory of a fish, the Putin government was rather quick in ordering an increase in the intensity of its air strikes again. The VKS thus continued the bombardment of insurgent-controlled Idlib province and, on 9 March 2016, also began bombing Daesh in the Palmyra area. Moscow reported 41 sorties as flown against targets in what once used to be the tourist pearl of Syria, and was still the biggest town in the Hamad, supposedly destroying no less than 146 targets. Meanwhile, all the available Ka-52s, Mi-28Ns, and most of the Mi-35Ms were forward deployed to Shayrat and T.4 ABs, from where they were able to reach the combat zone of Palmyra. However, with the Assad government lacking troops, it fell upon the IRGC-QF to re-deploy the necessary forces to central Syria. For this purpose, the Iranians dispatched most of the Liwa Fatemiyoun, Kata'ib Hezbollah, Harakat an-Nujba, Liwa Imam Ali, and at least another battalion of the Hezbollah/Lebanon. Supported by the VKS – but also by fighter-bombers and helicopters of the SyAAF, and by the FACs and combat engineers of the 61st Naval Infantry Brigade of the Russian Army – Axis forces managed to liberate Palmyra from the extremists on 27 March 2016. Daesh fought back viciously, leaving hundreds of improvised explosive devices (IEDs) in its trail, and occasionally launching counterattacks proceeded by so-called suicide vehicle-borne improvised explosive devices (SVBIEDs). When the extremists attempted to counterattack in the eastern Homs province, the VKS lost a Mi-28N underway on a nocturnal sortie: according to official reports from Moscow the helicopter 'flew into the ground', killing the crew of two, on 12 April 2016. The pilot of the helicopter in question was the commander of the Korenovsk-based 55th Helicopter Regiment, VKS.[130]

On 14 May 2016, the RGF experienced its next major mishap: VKS ground crews set afire a pile of empty wooden crates used to transport and store ammunition for helicopters forward deployed at T.4. Supported by strong wing prevalent in all of central Syria, the fire quickly went out of control and destroyed at least four Mi-24/35s. The resulting conflagration damaged not only an abandoned SyAAF MiG-25 parked nearby, but blew up about 20 trucks full of ammunition and other supplies, too. With Moscow never officially acknowledging such an accident – despite clear evidence in the form of reconnaissance satellite photographs published in the West – the full background of this incident, including the number of resulting casualties, remain unknown.[131]

T-72s operated by IRGC-QF's Liwa Fatimiyoun as seen during their deployment in the Palmyra area, in March 2016. (al-Mannar release)

A T-90 operated by IRGC-QF-controlled Liwa Assaib Ahl al-Haq seen in southern Aleppo, in March 2016. (al-Mannar release)

Failed Marriage

According to multiple statements by diverse representatives of the Putin government, the MOD in Moscow, the government of Bashar al-Assad, and the MOD in Damascus over the last three years, the GRF was 'fully coordinating' its operations with those of the government's military.[132] Similarly, at least for a majority of Western observers, Russia and Iran had been maintaining a close military alliance for decades.

The reality on the battlefields of Syria of mid-2016 was showing an entirely different picture: the VKS was continuously bombing towns like Darat Azza, Atarib, Hayyan, Hreitan, Anadan, Kfar Hamra, Ma'arat al-Artiq, and Urum al-Kubra in the western Aleppo and northern Idlib province; the SyAAF continued bombing civilians in the RTP, in Idlib, western and southern Aleppo, while a powerful concentration of Axis forces launched an offensive on Daesh in north-eastern Aleppo province, aiming to recover the Tabqa AB, perhaps even to reach Raqqa. Finally, a mix of IRGC-QF-controlled units was running its own campaign against Syrian insurgents and the JAN in southern Aleppo. In other words: each of the three parties supposed to fight 'for Assad' was running its own operations, entirely disconnected from each other. Unsurprisingly, the VKS campaign did little to support diverse Axis forces: the offensive on Tabqa was smashed by a single counterattack by Daesh, which sent most of the involved forces fleeing in panic back to Kweres AB; with the IRGC-QF-forces south of Aleppo experiencing another defeat at the hands of the JAF, and were pushed back by nearly 20 kilometres.

Apparently in an attempt to improve the coordination of their militaries, on 9 June 2016, the Iranian Minister of Defence,

Brigadier-General Hossein Dehghan, welcomed the Minister of Defence of the Russian Federation, General of the Army Sergey Kuzhugetovic Shoygu, and the Minister of Defence of the Syrian Arab Republic (and the Chief of the General Staff of the Armed Forces of Syria), Colonel-General Fahd Jassem al-Freij, for a meeting in Tehran. Although a conference of this kind was urgently necessary, except for the usual exchange of stereotypical diplomatic expressions, and obvious efforts to demonstrate friendship and harmony, its results remain unknown to this day. At most, they were of rather dubious quality, and resulting in several ironic affairs. The most famous amongst these was the deployment of six Tu-22M-3 and six Su-34s of the VKS to Nojeh AB, outside Hamedan, in western central Iran, on 15 August 2016. Originally agreed between the IRGC – genuinely keen to establish a strategic military alliance with the Russians – and Moscow, and expected by the Iranians to enable the VKS to provide better air support for Axis forces in Syria, this was a logical decision. However, eager to score propaganda points, the MOD in Moscow revealed the deployment of its bombers to Iran in public, while deploying these only into de-facto show attacks on Daesh-controlled areas in eastern Syria. Such behaviour proved to be based on particularly short-sighted decisions: Article 146 of the Constitution of the Islamic Republic of Iran strictly forbids the basing of foreign troops on Iranian soil, 'even for peaceful purposes'. Unsurprisingly, following ever louder complaints from multiple members of the Majlis (Iranian Parliament) and the Iranian public, the IRGC was forced to order the Russians out of Nojeh AB, on 23 August. Furthermore, while initially claiming the Majlis had nothing to say about this deployment, Dehghan subsequently turned to China for military cooperation.[133]

Battles for Castello Road and Ramousseh District

Despite their problems south of the city, the commanders of Axis forces had meanwhile sought for ways to close the siege of eastern Aleppo by an attack on the Castello Road – the last avenue of land communication into the city.[134] Organising such an enterprise proved anything other than easy because of massive differences within the 'pro Assad' camp: the Hindarat area selected as a springboard for this offensive was controlled by diverse Iranian-controlled militias, and the Liwa al-Qods al-Filistini, but Damascus demanded this offensive include the Tiger Force and at least one unit of the BPM – for propaganda purposes. With many of the Iranian-commanded combatants despising the forces of the Assad government almost as much as the insurgents did, even armed clashes between them and the Tiger Force were unavoidable, and had been reported on at least two occasions, on 15 and 16 June 2016.

Unsurprisingly, once the offensive was launched, on 25 June 2016, it advanced rather slowly, despite support from several artillery units of the Russian Army and the SyAAF. Eventually, it took the deployment of four Iraqi Shi'a militias, massive volumes of interdiction strikes by the SyAAF and the VKS on the roads connecting Aleppo with northern Idlib, and the cooperation of the YPG-contingent that was in control of Sheikh Maqsood District inside Aleppo City, to conclude it successfully, on 27 July 2016. With this, the insurgent-controlled parts of the city were cut off from the outside world.

A mere 24 hours later, following months-long negotiations and immense pressure from Turkey and Qatar, the JAN announced it was distancing itself from al-Qaeda, and its re-designation as the Jabhat Fateh ash-Sham (JFS). As soon as an appropriate statement was published, Turkey rushed numerous convoys carrying ammunition and supplies, and hundreds of foreign volunteers

A row of Tu-22M-3s of the VKS as seen parked on the Tarmac of Nojeh AB, in Iran, on 15 August 2016. Visible are (from front towards the rear), Borts 43, 16 and 57. Another example known to have been temporarily deployed to Iran during this operation was the Bort 42. (Russian Ministry of Defence)

One of the Tu-22M-3s deployed to Hamedan was 'Bort 57': this former mount of the Russian Naval Aviation was still wearing the 'sharkmouth' insignia as of August 2015. (Russian Ministry of Defence)

over the border to reinforce the JAF, which – as well as the JFS – now comprised insurgent groups like Ahrar ash-Sham (Syrian Salafists), Harakat Noureddin az-Zenghi (formerly supported by the USA, then leaning towards the Salafist ideology), Faylaq ash-Sham, Ajnad ash-Sham and the Central Division FSyA. Whether intentionally or by accident, once again the VKS and the SyAAF had completely failed to interrupt the resulting movement towards southern Aleppo. Indeed, when the JAF launched its counter-offensive, on 31 July 2016, this took by surprise even those Axis forces that were securing southern outskirts of the city. Unsurprisingly, on 3 August 2016, the JAF punched through and established contact to the insurgents inside eastern Aleppo and then widened the corridor into the besieged city to 2,200 metres.

The IRGC-QF reacted by rushing numerous Iraqi Shi'a militias to the frontlines, and deploying these into dilletantic counterattacks from multiple directions. The SyAAF provided close air support – mostly with L-39s, but also with Su-22s from Shayrat and Kweres (the latter began deploying ODAB-500ShL parachute-retarded thermobaric bombs of Russian origin during this period) – but suffered a series of losses. Mostly credited to technical malfunctions, these have shown that after ten months of intensive operations, its fighter-bomber fleet was in need of maintenance. The Russians reacted with indifference: Moscow and the HQ of the GRF had meanwhile reduced the number of VKS fighter bombers deployed at Hmeimim, and instead launched another round of bombing eastern Syria with Tu-22M-3s from Mozdok AB. On 11 July 2016, two Russian bombers plastered a camp housing about 50,000 refugees from Palmyra, stranded close to the Jordanian border because the authorities in Amman forbade them the entry: dozens of civilians were killed. Further air strikes by Tu-22M-3s were flown on 8 August (six bombers), 11 August (six bombers), 14 August (two bombers) and 16 August (six Tu-22 that operated from Iran), but it remains unknown what exactly these had attempted to hit.

Thus, it was on the IRGC-QF to solve the problem in southern Aleppo. Following the failure of costly counterattacks into the Ramousseh District, somebody in the Glasshouse came up with a better idea: an offensive further south, from the area of al-Bhurfah towards Khan Touman, over the open terrain outside the city of Aleppo, where the IRGC-QF and its proxies could exploit their superior fire-power, while the other side lacked cover. This solution proved far more effective: not only in that it outmanoeuvred

the JAF positions in southern Aleppo, forcing the insurgents and jihadists into a rushed withdrawal, but it also re-sealed the siege of the eastern part of the city, between 4 and 6 September 2016. By then, both sides had suffered extensive losses: up to 900 insurgents (primarily from Idlib) and transnational jihadists, and about 550 combatants of the Axis forces were killed, while the combined loss of armoured vehicles was well in excess of 50. That was at least 10 percent of the involved fighters and heavy weaponry deployed by each side in this battle.[135]

BMP-1s and T-72s of the JFS during the advance into southern Aleppo in June 2016. Although Hmeimim AB was only 60-120 kilometres away from this battlefield, the VKS failed to strike any of the lengthy columns bringing heavy equipment, supplies and thousands of insurgents into position. (Ahrar ash-Sham release)

A Tu-22M-3 releasing a string of 10 OFAB-250-270 bombs over eastern Syria, in July or August 2016. Several such strikes hit the IDP camps, containing most of Palmyra's population, in the desert close to the Jordanian border. (Russian Ministry of Defence)

Insurgents of Ahrar ash-Sham inside southern suburbs of Aleppo City in July 2016. (Ahrar ash-Sham release)

Kneel or Starve

By 2016, there was no doubt about the widespread application of the policy characterised as 'kneel or starve' – after graffiti scrawled during one of the raids by security services of the Assad government across Syria in 2011-2012 – by the Axis forces all around Syria. Indeed, by then the essence of the Syrian War became about 40 large-scale, years-long sieges of major urban areas: with three exceptions, all of these were maintained by the 'pro-Assad' camp. Although most of those besieged were non-combatants, the forces controlled by the Assad government, the IRGC-QF, and the GRF insisted on treating everybody inside as 'combatants' – or at least: 'guilty, until proven innocent'. In August 2016, the four-year siege of Darayya, a district of Damascus that 'dared' challenging the Assad government the most, was forced into submission through a combination of starvation and massive bombardment by all means – including VKS air strikes: survivors agreed to be evacuated to Idlib, and the area subsequently declared an (Iranian-controlled) 'military zone'. This 'success' emboldened the Axis commanders to apply the same methods elsewhere, especially in Aleppo. The assault on besieged civilians during the last months of the battle for that city thus reached dimensions not experienced since 1945.[136]

Facing a growing international critique, Moscow agreed to impose several cease-fires, and permit delivery of relief aid to the beleaguered part of the city, in September 2016. However, none of the cease-fires was respected and no aid was delivered: the Axis forces did their best to spoil any such agreements. One typical atrocity committed during this period took place on the evening of 19 September 2016, when a UN and World Food Programme-sponsored convoy of 31 trucks hauling relief aid from Turkey reached the base of the Syrian Association of the Red Crescent (SARC) in Urum al-Kubra, about 12 kilometres outside the city. Although Damascus was well-informed about this enterprise and granted a safe passage, shortly after its arrival in Urum al-Kubra the convoy was subjected to a series of devastating air strikes that killed 20 civilians – including the director of the SARC, Omar Barakat – and destroyed 18 trucks. While some of the involved SyAAF crews subsequently boasted about 'destroying a Nusra convoy' in the social media, officially Damascus and Moscow did their best to deny their involvement, amongst others by stressing that the SyAAF was not capable of flying air strikes by night.[137] As so often, the reality was entirely different.

One of the primary reasons for the Assad government's drive to lift the siege of Kweres AB was the necessity to free up to 50 cadets of the Air Force Academy, locked-up there since 2012, but now urgently needed to replace war-time losses of the SyAAF. Almost immediately afterwards, selected student pilots underwent refresher training and then began training operations by night. Also freed at Kweres AB in November 2015 were numerous training jets: out of 55 L-39ZO and 44 L-39ZA armed trainers Syria had purchased from the former Czechoslovakia in the 1970s and 1980s, less than 25 were left intact by 2016, and thus any reinforcements were most welcome. By mid-2016, up to 22 of these were rushed through overhauls at 'The Works' – the SyAAF's major overhaul facility at Nayrab AB (military side of Aleppo International) – during which most were modified to carry two B-8M rocket pods, each packing a hefty punch of 18 S-8

unguided 80mm rockets. Other examples could still carry either bombs of up to 250 kilograms, or UB-16-57 rocket pods, while surviving L-39ZAs retained their twin-barrel 23mm cannon installed under the fuselage. By April 2016, six modified L-39s were grouped into a night-attack unit of the SyAAF, commanded by Colonel Youssef al-Hassan. As soon as their training was complete, they went into action – primarily in the form of attacks on the traffic along the Castello Road by night. By September 2016, there were regular reports about 'machine-gun-armed-jets'

A Shi'a 'Mullah' and a group of IRGC-QF's 'pilgrims' praying inside ruined Darayya, once this district of Damascus was abandoned by local insurgents and most of these – and most of the local population – deported to Idlib in August 2016. (IRGC-QF release)

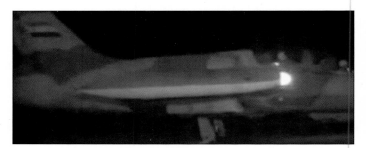

While entirely missed in the West, the media controlled by the Assad government began reporting about the training of SyAAF L-39 crews in nocturnal operations as early as of November 2015 – shortly after the siege of Kweres AB was lifted. This still from a video released by the Syrian Arab News Agency (SANA) was released around the same time. (SANA)

One of the L-39s modified to carry B-8M pods for S-8K unguided 80mm rockets, as seen at Tiyas AB (T.4), in December 2015. (via R. S.)

attacking the same area, then Ramousseh District, and then eastern Aleppo: two thirds of these by L-39s launched from Kweres AB between 1600 and 1800hrs local time, the remaining third from Hama, Nayrab and Tiyas air bases. Regardless of how much the governments in Damascus and Moscow denied all the charges and instead put the blame on somebody else, it was the L-39 of Hassan's unit that played the crucial role in the destruction of the UN-convoy at Urum al-Kubra, during the night of 19 September 2016: they deployed FAB-OFAB-250-270 bombs, unguided rockets and internal cannons during that attack.[138]

Air Strikes on Hospitals

The destruction of the UN-convoy in Urum al-Kubra was no exception. On the contrary, it was a part of the campaign characterised by sustained attacks on civilian facilities, especially hospitals, mostly those inside besieged eastern Aleppo, and especially those supported by Western NGOs, for reasons explained earlier. Certainly enough, the 'hospitals' in question were often anything other than what would deserve that name in the West, for example: they were either diverse re-purposed buildings, or underground installations equipped to provide different degrees of medical assistance. While the Kremlin's propaganda-machinery attempted to distract from operations against such facilities with a smear campaign aimed at declaring their staff, but especially members of the Syrian Civil Defence, as 'al-Qaeda', the VKS had several times deployed BETAB-500 concrete-piercing 'bunker busters', and also RBK-500 CBUs filled with thermite-based incendiaries against them: for example, between 5 June and 10 August 2016, the HRW reported the use of such weapons in at least 18 air strikes on opposition-controlled areas of Aleppo and Idlib. A further nine cases were reported in September. Moscow reacted with ridiculous denial: Major-General Igor Konashenkov, the spokesman of the MOD, explicitly denied the use of incendiary weapons and declared all the related accusations as being based on fake evidence and clichés – and this after the Kremlin-controlled satellite channel RT repeatedly published videos showing RBK-500s filled with ZAB-2.5S/M incendiary bombs installed on a Su-34 at Hmeimim AB, during the visit by the Russian defence minister Shoygu, on 18 June 2016.[139]

Furthermore, between June and December of the same year, no less than 172 attacks on medical facilities in parts of Syria controlled by the insurgents or the JAN were documented by the World Health Organization (WHO), Physicians for Human Rights, Médicins Sans Frontières (MSF), and Amnesty International (AI): 73 verified attacks were recorded inside besieged eastern Aleppo (one of the hospitals in the besieged part of the city was hit no less than 12 times during that period).[140] Exactly how many related air strikes were flown by the VKS remains unknown. Moscow has denied its involvement, although it is certain that the Russian fighter-bombers had participated at least in the nocturnal air strikes on eastern Aleppo – as obvious from the widespread deployment of CBUs filled with thermite incendiary ammunition of types never used by the SyAAF, such as RBK-500 ZAB-2.5S/M or RBK-500 PTAB-1M. Ironically, deployment of such weapons ceased only after Shoygu announced the termination of (VKS) air strikes against targets in Aleppo, on 18 October 2016.[141]

Russian Minister of Defence Shoygu (third from left), with top commanders of the GRF in front of a Su-35S fighter-bomber at Hmeimim AB on 16 June 2016. (Russian Ministry of Defence)

On 16 November 2016, strategic bombers of the VKS flew their second round of cruise missile strikes against targets in Syria – primarily in Idlib and western Aleppo. This photograph of the Tu-95MS Bort '11 Red/Vorkuta', was taken during one of missions in question. (Russian Ministry of Defence)

The importance of cruise-missile air strikes on insurgent-controlled parts of north-western Syria grew in 2016 due to the emergence of a well-organized network of ground observers that began announcing VKS and SyAAF air strikes to the population in Syria: the locals had no means of receiving timely warnings about cruise-missile attacks. This photograph of the Tu-160 Bort '12 Red/Aleksandr Novikov' was taken while the bomber was underway to Syria in November 2016. (Russian inistry of Defence)

Eventually, in the period September-December 2016, eastern Aleppo was subjected to a total of 823 registered air strikes, resulting in the release of about 4,000 bombs. These caused the death of at least 4,000 civilians – although it should be kept in mind that these figures include only the registered fatalities, confirmed by multiple sources: the number of bodies left under the ruins of the city remains unknown.[142]

Betrayed Offensive

As well as the idea of being involved in a proxy war with the USA, at least a part of such behaviour by the MOD in Moscow and the VKS in Syria can be described as 'caused by frustration': by the end of 2016, the Russians had managed to track down and kill only a handful of insurgent, few JAN, and not a single Daesh commander. Indeed, when – in mid-October 2016, multiple large columns of the JAF coalition once again moved from diverse points around the Idlib province in a western direction – the GRF failed to detect, track and attack any of these. For example: while the Central Division FSyA moved a column of dozens of its vehicles and hundreds of combatants in broad daylight, on 26 October, SyAAF Su-22s from Shayrat bombed a school in the town of Hass, in Idlib, using ODAB-500 fuel-air-explosive bombs, killing at least 22 children and six teachers in one of the worst single attacks on civilians in that year. Simultaneously, VKS Su-24s were bombing Kfar Nabl in southern Idlib, while the SyAAF then bombed the HQ of what was meanwhile Faylaq Homs (former Jaysh at-Tawhid), in the RTP, killing four of its commanders, including Colonel Shoqi Ayoub Abo Ibrahim, and his deputy, Lieutenant-Colonel Faysal Awdh.[143]

Later, on the same day, a highly interesting photograph appeared in the social media controlled by the Assad government, showing the military commander of Aleppo, Major-General Zaid Saleh, with Mohammad Jaber, owner of the Liwa Suqour as-Sahra. Behind the officers was a map revealing that the Syrian military intelligence was well informed about the JAF's planning for the offensive into western Aleppo: it clearly showed multiple blue arrows – denoting intended directions of attack – through the al-Assad and Districts 1070 and 3000, in the direction of the city's besieged eastern half. Combined, these events have once again illustrated that the HQ GRF was receiving next to no substantial intelligence. Indeed, that even the deployment of about 70 surveillance drones – ranging from large Yakovlev Pchela-1 to small Orlan-10s, Eleron-3SVs and Granat-4s – was insufficient to provide them with better insights into the developments deeper within insurgent-controlled territories.[144] Instead, the Russians in Syria of mid-2016 only knew what the intelligence services of the Assad government wanted them to know.

The JAF thus launched its offensive on 28 October with a series of stunning attacks proceeded by SVBIEDs. By 1 November, it captured three districts and approached to within 2,000 metres of insurgent lines inside eastern Aleppo. However, subsequent flow of this battle has shown that this offensive took only the IRGC and the Russians by surprise: by 3 November, counterattacks by the Tiger Force and the Liwa Suqour as-Sahra had caused heavy losses to the JFS in particular, and eventually forced the entire coalition into a withdrawal – and then one that resulted not only in the collapse of this coalition, but also in infighting between the transnational jihadists and multiple Syrian insurgent groups. With this, the last attempt to lift the siege of eastern Aleppo failed – even without the VKS, which appeared on the scene only towards the end of this battle, and then in the form of air strikes on insurgent and jihadist positions in the western outskirts of the city. Supported by its own UAVs, during the last week of November, the IRGC-QF's and forces of the Assad government had pushed into the suburb of Hanano, and then split the enclave in eastern Aleppo in two. Security forces of the Assad government followed on their heels: sorting out, detaining and executing those who were caught, and widespread looting began almost immediately. While related reports were difficult to substantiate, they did prompt the GRF to deploy Russian Military Police in the city once the fighting was over, in an attempt to curb such behaviour.[145]

One of the new appearances on the battlefields of Syria during the final battle for Aleppo were BRDM-2 armoured cars, mounting ZU-23 twin-barrel, 23mm anti-aircraft cannon, like this example. Reportedly, such vehicles – and also specially modified BRDM-2s that served to transport FACs – were operated by the Russian troops only. (Syrian social media)

A rare photograph of a Tu-214R – probably the second prototype, registration RF-64514, known to have been deployed at Hmeimim AB since July 2016 – underway over Aleppo, on 6 October 2016, while escorted by at least one Su-30SM. (Syrian social media)

Air strikes by the SyAAF – foremost flown by helicopters forward deployed at the newly-constructed helidrome of as-Safira – were meanwhile relentless, but the insurgents did manage to shoot down at least one of the aircraft involved: early during the evening of 3 December 2016, the L-39 flown by Lieutenant-Colonel Abboud Hassan and Captain Tarek Muwaffaq M'alla was shot down over eastern Aleppo, and its crew killed. Subsequently, organized resistance began to crumble due to a series of air strikes that resulted in the deployment of chemical weapons. By 13 December only five percent of eastern Aleppo was still controlled by the opposition. Amid the ensuing chaos, over 135,000 civilians sought refuge within areas nominally controlled by the Assad government before an evacuation of about 50,000 survivors – primarily civilians but including up to 8,000 members of multiple insurgent groups – was negotiated to start on the morning of the following day. Interrupted time and again – especially by IRGC-QF-controlled units that felt unconcerned by related agreements – this process lasted longer than a week. On 22 December 2016, jubilant Damascus declared all of Aleppo as under its control.[146]

Second Russian 'Withdrawal'

Some of the Russian air strikes against northern Idlib and western Aleppo in November and December 2016 were flown by the air group nominally embarked aboard the aircraft carrier *Admiral Flota Sovetskogo Soyuza Kuznetsov*. The carrier and her strike group (including nuclear battle cruiser *Pyotr Veliky*, destroyers *Severomorsk*

A Su-30SM of the VKS overflying Kuznetsov off the Syrian coast in November 2016. (Russian Ministry of Defence)

and *Vice-Admiral Kulakov*, and five support ships) reached the Syrian coast following a lengthy voyage from Severomorsk, via the English Channel and Gibraltar. Consisting of 10 Su-33 and 5 MiG-29KUB/R fighter-bombers, 2 Ka-27PL/PS anti-submarine helicopters, 2 Ka-29TB and 1 Ka-52K attack helicopters, and 2 Ka-31 early warning helicopters, the air group commenced combat operations starting on 15 November 2016. Bad weather and lack of experience in running an aircraft carrier at war quickly converted the entire effort into a failure, as two fighters were lost in landing-related accidents, revealing a major problem with *Kuznetsov's* arrestor gear. Eventually, all the fighter-bombers were disembarked to Hmeimim AB, and flew the majority of their sorties from the ground. According to the MOD in Moscow, the air group flew 420 sorties over Syria, including 117 by night: however, NATO subsequently reported that only 154 sorties were made from the carrier. Nevertheless, the Russian naval aviation was (and remains at the time of writing) involved in combat operations in Syria in diverse other forms, foremost through the continuous rotation of its land-based aircraft and crews to the Aviation Group based at Hmeimim AB.[147]

The fall of eastern Aleppo was the second decisive moment for crushing the insurgency in Syria. Unsurprisingly, the jubilant Putin government exploited the opportunity to announce – yet another

– 'withdrawal' of the Russian military from Syria (including at least eight Su-24M fighter-bombers), on 29 December 2016. As so often before and after, none of the related statements could have been more distant from reality: except for the *Kuznetsov's* air group (which ceased flying operations over Syria on 5 January 2017) only 12 VKS fighter-bombers were actually sent back home – and promptly replaced by four Su-25SM-3s.[148]

Deck crew preparing FAB-500M-54 general purpose bombs for installation on the MiG-29KUB fighter-bomber visible in the background. Less well-equipped than Su-35S', Su-34s and Su-30SMs of the VKS, Sukhois and MiGs deployed to Syria by Kuznetsov were even more reliant on so-called 'dumb', or 'free fall' bombs. (Russian Ministry of Defence)

CHAPTER 5
DECISIVE BATTLE

Despite the victory of their allies in Aleppo, the year 2017 began rather unpleasantly for the Russians in Syria. Differences between their leadership and Iranian top commanders had reportedly reached such proportions, that they might have lead to an IRGC-QF-supported coup-attempt by Maher al-Assad in Damascus of January 2017. In February, the Russians found themselves involved in the next crisis with Turkey, which meanwhile launched its own intervention in Syria, and liberated the town of al-Bab from Daesh

– in turn preventing the establishment of a land corridor between the PKK/PYD/YPG/YPJ-controlled Afrin enclave, and the SDF-controlled north-eastern Syria. Supposedly keen to effect an end to fighting, Moscow opened intensive negotiations with the USA, Turkey and diverse other foreign powers: however, the resulting cease-fire of 27 February 2017 quickly failed because the VKS never stopped bombing civilians in Idlib and Eastern Ghouta. On the contrary, the Russian behaviour provoked several major insurgent counter-attacks. Furthermore, still essentially untouched by the Russian military, Moscow's declared objective in Syria – Daesh – launched an offensive into the centre of Syria, overran Palmyra and reached the perimeter of the T.4 and Dmeyr air bases.[149]

It is notable that the contemporary reactions of the Putin government, and those of the HQ GRF, were rather slow, reluctant, and frequently left the impression that they were keen to let their Syrian and Iranian allies lose – along the lines of the motto, 'don't tell me I didn't tell you'.

Rebuff in Palmyra

Exploiting the preoccupation of the Assad government and the IRGC-QF with the battle for Aleppo, on the evening of 9 December 2016 Daesh deployed a group of about 400 extremists for a lightning attack on Palmyra. Combining multiple SVBIEDs with tanks and small columns of light vehicles, it shocked, panicked and overran the outlying positions and then drove right into the local air base and the town. Paradoxically the HQ GRF did recognize the incoming threat, but instead of reinforcing defenders only ordered the withdrawal of the local Russian garrison. Left on their own, the remaining defenders – comprising two battalions of militias loyal to the Assad government, corseted by a detachment from the Tiger Force – followed in fashion and ran away, leaving behind 16 intact MBTs, 6 BMP-1s, numerous other vehicles and huge amounts of ammunition and supplies. Emboldened, the Daesh then pushed further west and attacked the T.4 AB: once again, the Russians beat a hasty retreat, withdrawing four Su-25s forward deployed there. On the other hand, throughout this period, the VKS continued bombing insurgents and civilians in the Idlib province.[150]

Moscow and the HQ GRF did very little even on 15 January 2017, when Daesh launched an all-out attack on the besieged garrison of Assad government forces in the city of Dayr az-Zawr: proceeded by several SVBIEDs, this assault nearly overran the local air base, destroyed two L-39s on the ground, captured an operational 2K12 Kub (ASCC-code 'SA-6 Gainful') SAM-site, and split the government-controlled pocket into two. Certainly enough, Mozdok-based Tu-22M-3s were sent into action over eastern Syria, and flew a round of air strikes between 21 and 25 January 2017, while the Aviation Group at Hmeimim AB was reinforced through four additional Su-34s and four Su-25SM-3s. However, all of these measures had shown no effects upon the

operations of the extremists: the only Russian measure that could be described as 'effective' against the Daesh during this period, was the forward deployment of attack helicopters at Shayrat AB, and then – once the threat of this base getting overrun by the Daesh was diminished – at T.4 AB. The extremists then re-directed their efforts and punched further west: although failing to capture Dmeyr AB, they did manage to cause heavy losses to the locally-based SyAAF units and cut off this crucial facility from the outside world for weeks.[151]

Drive on Hama

Following the failure of the cease-fire of 27 February 2017, an attack of the VKS on Turkish troops near al-Bab, and after repeated massacres of civilians in Idlib by the bombs of the SyAAF and the VKS, in early March, the Erdogan government made the decision to bolster its support for the insurgency in Idlib. It not only granted permission for several large units to re-deploy from the Turkish-controlled pocket around al-Bab to Idlib, but literally flooded them with supplies. The FSyA and the HTS thus exploited the opportunity to launch an offensive on the city of Hama, following a plan developed two years earlier, which – by sheer accident – was prevented by the start of the Russian military intervention. According to that plan, reorganized FSyA units including Jaysh al-Azza, Jaysh Idlib, and Jaysh an-Nasir, attacked out of the Lataminah Salient towards south on the western flank, while the HTS meanwhile – including the Turkistan Islamic Party (HQ in Jishr ash-Shughour) – attacked in the direction of Hama via Moarek on the eastern flank.

Although at least the intelligence services of the Assad government were tipped-off about this offensive on time, Damascus could do very little to pre-empt it. The reason was that the blow hit an area that was meanwhile outside its control: the HQ of 11th Division was dysfunctional, while – with less than a handful of exceptions – the local warlords either pledged loyalty to the IRGC, or to Maher al-Assad, or declared themselves independent from any kind of higher authorities. Apparently attempting to pre-empt the coming attack, the SyAAF flew intensive air strikes on Idlib, Sarqib and Kfar Zita, starting with 16 March, and an attack of two Su-24MK2s on the HQ of the Jaysh Idlib, two days later. However, this proved insufficient – even more so because the VKS continued its random bombing of northern Idlib and western Aleppo.[152]

Free to concentrate their forces undisturbed, insurgent and HTS commanders had initiated their offensive during the afternoon of 21 March, under the cover of bad weather. The FSyA units literally sliced through two defensive lines of diverse militias. Within 48 hours, they reached the village of Arzeh, only three kilometres outside Hama AB. However, contrary to the original plan, the HTS concentrated all of its efforts for an assault of the heavily fortified village of Qamahana, where local militias were meanwhile reinforced by the Harakat an-Nujba and various other IRGC-QF proxies. Thus, the advance came to a stand-still: when the weather improved, on 23 March, the VKS flew no less than 108 air strikes. For the first time ever in the course of the Russian military intervention in Syria, the majority of these targeted the HTS between Sarqib and Moarek. Furthermore, and whether by accident or design, several of the VKS' air strikes had ravaged the positions of the pro-Maher militia Tigers of Qamahana,

This Tu-22M-3 was photographed while releasing a load of six FAB-500M-62s somewhere over eastern Syria in early 2017. Note the wing spread fully forward, indicating slow speed of the bomber – necessary to improve the precision of its attack with help of the SVP-24 nav/attack system. (Russian Ministry of Defence)

The first batch of Mi-24s deployed by the VKS to Syria consisted of Mi-24Ds and Mi-24Ps equiped with no advanced self-protection systems, often even lacking standard flare dispensers and L166V infra red jammers on the rear side of the engine cowling. All were camouflaged in two shades of green on top surfaces and sides, and a bright light blue on undersurfaces, and wore two-digit 'Bort' numbers applied in yellow. Registrations and service titles were removed on arrival at Hmeimim AB, and borts were subsequently often decreased to only one digit. They were replaced by a batch of Mi-24Ps painted in dark sand and olive green, some of which wore very large borts in red (outlined in white). More advanced Mi-35Ms, equipped with the GSh-23V twin-barrel 23mm cannon, Vitebsk self-protection system, and exhaust diffusers began appearing only later in 2016. (Artwork by Tom Cooper)

The first four Mi-28Ns were confirmed as being deployed to Syria in March 2016, and it is certain that they saw lots of action against Daesh in eastern Syria. All wore the camouflage pattern shown here, consisting of dark sand and olive-green colours on top surfaces and sides, and light admiralty grey (BS381C/698) on undersurfaces. All four have received big Borts, in blue, outlined in white, underneath the pilot's (rear) cockpit – indicating their assignement to a test unit – while their registration-numbers were deleted, as shown here. In addition to the single-barrel 30mm 2A42-2 cannon, with 250 rounds, installed under the nose, they were usually armed with up to eight 9M120 Ataka-VN anti-tank missiles and B-8V-20A rocket packs. (Artwork by Tom Cooper)

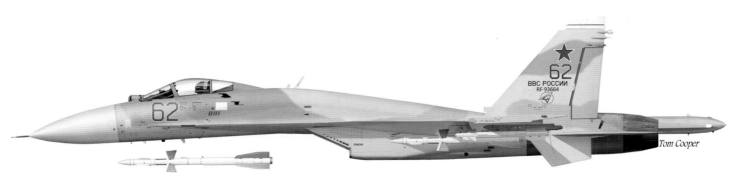

Sometime in summer 2017, the VKS deployed up to six Su-27SMs to Hmeimim AB. All were camouflaged in the standard pattern for that variant, consisting of light grey overall (FS 35550), with a disruptive scheme in blue-grey (FS 35420) and medium grey (FS 35526). All dielectric panels were painted in traffic white. Primarily serving as interceptors, these still had R-27R air-to-air missiles as their major armament. Gauging by mission markings – applied in the form of bomb silhouettes in red – each of them flew up to 50-60 combat missions before returning to Russia. (Artwork by Tom Cooper)

The first four Su-35S – widely considered the most advanced heavy, long-range multirole fighter of the VKS – were deployed to Hmeimim AB in January 2016, and were drawn from the Privolzhskiy AB's 18th Aviation Centre/116th Training Centre. Additional batches have been rotated through Syria ever since, so that most of the examples that served there collected about 150-170 mission markings. Red or white stars were applied above the latter, for uknown reasons. Their armament consisted of general-purpose bombs and RBKs, R-27Rs and R-73s early on: R-77 became more common only in mid-2016. While L005 Sorbstiya-series wingtip ECM-pods were used early on, by early 2018 the latest KNIRTI SAP-518 ECM-pods (illustrated here, and analogue to the ALQ-99 of the Boeing EA-18G Growler) appear to have become more common. (Artwork by Tom Cooper)

The first batch of Su-34s deployed to Syria included aircraft with Borts 20, 21, 22, and 23; 25, 27, and a few others became evident by November 2015. All were painted in dark grey on top surfaces and sides (this colour tended to bleach quite quickly), with an 'anti-glare panel' in black-green in front of the cockpit. All the undersurfaces were in light green-blue, while radomes and dielectric panels were painted in traffic white. All of their national insignia, and most of registration-numbers were crudely overpainted (apparently with a brush) with dark grey. Mission markings – in the form of red stars applied below the front cockpit – began appearing in November 2015. This example ('22 Red', RF-95005) is shown with a weapons configuration including a pair each of R-73s, R-27Rs, KAB-500Krs, and FAB-250M-62s. Insets show other commonly deployed weapons, including (from left towards right): FAB-500M-62, BetAB-500, KAB-500Kr, ODAB-500, RBK-500AO-2.5RT, RBK-500AB-2.5, RBK-500SPBE-D, and RKB-500U (all seen 'in action' in Syria). (Artwork by Tom Cooper)

An even larger number of Su-34s deployed at Hmeimim AB, starting from November 2015, wore this camouflage pattern, consisting of light blue-green, medium blue-green and dark blue-green on top surfaces (with a big 'anti-glare panel' applied in black-green in front of the cockpit), and light blue-green on undersurfaces. Many had their radomes and diverse panels painted in traffic white, while others had them painted in fog grey. Top inset is shown the front part of the Su-34 assigned to the Akhtubinsk State Flight Test Centre (known as Valery Chkalov 929 GLIT), as worn by at least one of aircraft deployed at Hmeimim AB starting in March 2016. Below 'Red 02' are KAB-500S-E and KAB-1500LG (left side), and Kh-38MA anti-ship missile (sighted several times under Su-34s in Syria of 2016 and 2017). (Artworks by Tom Cooper)

The designation Su-30 is actually used for an entire family of heavy fighter-bombers that was widely exported. The Su-30SM is an Irkutsk-manufactured variant, custom-tailored for the VKS, equipped with the RLSU-30MK-R Bars-R (N001M-R) radar, with Indian-made computers, the French Thales HUD3022 (expected to be replaced by the Russian IKSh-1M on the SM-3), and the Russian IFF-system and L-150 Pastel RWR. The aircraft that arrived in Syria in September 2015 had their national insignia crudely overpainted, while service titles were re-applied two months later. They were frequently equipped with the KNIRTI SAP-518 wingtip ECM-pods, but still lacked R-77s: a batch of these was hurriedly acquired and deployed only after the downing of the Su-24. In early 2018, a batch of Su-30SMs of the Naval Aviation was sighted as deployed at Hmeimim AB, including the Bort '47 Blue' illustrated in the inset (Notably, they wore the corresponding service title on their fins and the Russian Navy's ensign behind the rear cockpit). By that time, obsolete R-27Rs were almost completely replaced by R-77s. (Artworks by Tom Cooper)

After the Su-24, the Su-25 was the second 'workhorse' of the VKS in Syria. While the initial batch of 12 aircraft included earlier Su-25SMs (mostly Su-25SM-76s), by 2017 the most advanced Su-25SM-3s had also appeared at Hmeimim AB, two of which are illustrated here. The primary means of outside identification of this sub-variant are minimal changes in regards of the antenna configuration behind the cockpit: most of SM-3s identified so far have received an antenna related to the Metronome communications system. Another detail often reported as related to Su-25SM-3s is a small housing on the lower part of the front fuselage, and the appearance of L-370-3S ECM-pods (shown in inset, in lower right corner), always carried on the outermost underwing hardpoints (instead of pylons for R-60/AA-8 missiles). Their camouflage patterns consisted of beige (BS381C/388), green (FS24138) and brown (usually FS20111, but sometimes FS30045 or FS30219). (Artworks by Tom Cooper)

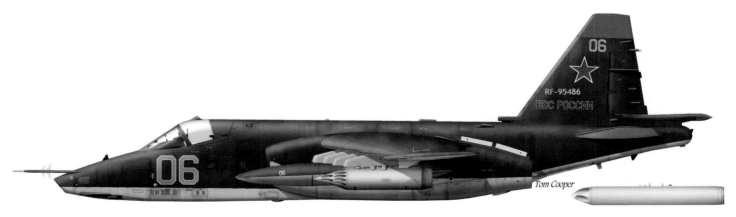

This is a reconstruction of the Su-25SM Bort '06 Blue' (RF-95486) shot down on 3 February 2018 over southern Idlib, while flown by Major Roman Filipov. Contrary to some of the fleet, this and plenty of other Su-25s deployed to Syria were painted in the same dark grey on top surfaces and sides as some of the Su-34s. Originally drawn from the Chernigovka-based 187th Guards Attack Aviation Squadron, this aircraft arrived at Hmeimim AB sometime in December 2017, during the third (and 'final') withdrawal announced by President Putin. It is shown as usually configured during this period: including drop tanks on the inboard underwing pylons, and one or two B-8M pods for unguided rockets. Also deployed in combat in Syria were the less-well known B-13 pods for five 130mm rockets, one of which is shown in the lower right corner. (Artwork by Tom Cooper)

All the Su-24s of the VKS are painted in medium grey (FS 73092) on top surfaces and sides, and dielectric white (FS 73125) on the radome, undersides, and diverse dielectric pannels, whereas the front border of the latter is applied in differing positions ahead of the cockpit. The aircraft shown here was the example shot down by the THK's F-16C on 24 November 2015. It is illustrated with the last known number of mission markings (five red stars), partially re-applied national markings and service titles, and as armed with a total of six FAB-250-270 bombs. (Artwork by Tom Cooper)

Heavy use, exposure to the Syrian sun and sand, and the salt of the nearby Mediterranean Sea usually bleached the medium grey colour on top surfaces and sides of all the Su-24Ms at Hmeimim AB. In turn, the longer the intervention went on, the more mission markings were added by their ground crews: already by mid-2016, several aircraft were showing up to 40 of these (standing for over 400 combat sorties flown). Bort '49 White' (top artwork) is representative of the second batch deployed in Syria, while Bort '11 White' was sighted later in 2016. Although capable of carrying much heavier loads, the type flew most of their sorties armed with only four bombs of 250 or 500kg. The examples here are shown carrying BetAB-500s (top) and RBK-500AO-2.5RTs. (Artworks by Tom Cooper)

Perhaps the biggest surprise of the entire Russian military intervention in Syria was a week-long deployment of at least two (according to unsubstantiated reports: up to four) prototypes of the Sukhoi T-50 PAK-FA (officially designated the 'Su-57' in December 2017), in February 2018. Hushed-up by Moscow and essentially pointless because hardly any of these had an operational weapons system, the motivation for this enterprise might have been a last-ditch attempt to prevent the ultimate Indian cancellation of further funding for this project, which followed a few weeks later. The examples comfirmed as deployed to Syria were the T-50-10 (Bort '510 Blue') and T-50-11, shown here (RF-81775, first flown only on 5 August 2017!). Although Moscow subsequently released a video showing one of these releasing a guided missile, it seems that neither of the two aircraft fired a single shot in Syria. (Artwork by Tom Cooper)

Time and again, the VKS has concentrated up to 25 Tu-22M-3 bombers from all of its operational units – or more than a third of its entire fleet – for operations in Syria. Six of them were forward deployed at Nojeh AB in Iran in August 2016. Whether originally acquired by the VKS, or former mounts of the Naval Aviation (like the example shown on the main artwork here, Bort '57 Red', RF-34079) all the aircraft were painted in the same medium grey on upper surfaces and sides, and dielectric white on lower surfaces. Some of the former Naval Aviation aircraft still show their 'sharkmouth' insignia, first seen in the mid-2000s, while at least one Tu-22M-3 (Bort '24 Red', RF-95154' shown in inset) was named after 'Mikhail Shidovsky'. Their principal weapons for attacks on Syria consisted of OFAB-250-270 and FAB-500M-62 bombs, but at least one FAB-3000M54 – probably the biggest conventional weapon of the Syrian War at 3000kg – was deployed too. (Artwork by Tom Cooper)

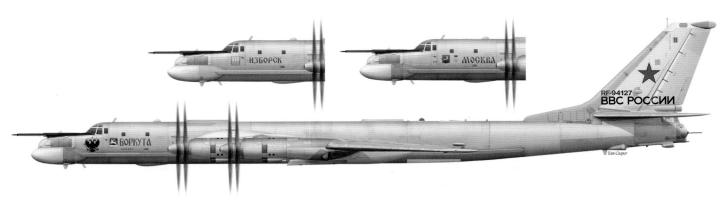

In November 2015, no less than 59 years after entering service, Tu-95s saw their first ever combat. Only a few details are known about a dozen examples deployed for cruise-missile attacks on Syria in November 2015 and November 2016. Two of the Tu-95SM-1s identified as involved on the latter occasion were Bort '11 Red/Vorkuta/RF-94127' (subsequently sighted wearing mission markings for 60 sorties, as shown on the illustration here) and Bort '27 Red/Izborsk/RF-94117', while Bort '12 Red/Moskva/RF-94126' (but also Bort '19 Red/Krasnoyarsk/RF-94123', RF-94131 and RF-94218) may have been involved in earlier operations. Their primary weapons were Kh-555 cruise missiles, two carried in pairs on each of four underwing pylons. (Artworks by Tom Cooper)

The Tu-214R is a little-known multi-role reconnaissance aircraft, only two prototypes of which were undergoing trials as of November 2015, when the first of them – the example shown here, registration RF-64511 – was deployed to Syria. The primary mission equipment of this variant consists of the Vega MRK-411 multi-band radar system, which includes side-looking radars with flat antennas on the forward fuselage, and an all-round surveillance radar in a teardrop-shaped radome under the aft fuselage. The long fairing under the forward fuselage houses a high-definiton electro-optical reconnaissance system that works in two bands, visible and infra-red, and includes multiple digital and thermal imaging cameras. Painted in light admiralty grey overall (except for the sat-com antenna on the back of the aircraft, which is painted in radome white), both aircraft were only marked with the national flag and their registrations. (Artwork by Tom Cooper)

The Beriev A-50U is an upgrade of the A-50 strategic airborne early warning aircraft based on the airframe of the Ilyushin Il-76MD. The centrepiece of this variant is the E-821 Shmel radar, with the range of 300-350km (186-218 miles) for large targets flying at high altitude, and the capability of simultaneously tracking 45 targets, the antenna of which is housed inside the typical radome atop a pedestal over the rear fuselage. Out of about 24 originally manufactured A-50s, some 19 remain in service. The first of them was deployed to Syria in reaction to the US TLAM-strike on Shayrat AB in May 2017. Since December of the same year, up to two A-50Us were forward deployed at Hmeimim AB. Illustrated here is Bort '41 Red' (outlined in blue), nick-named 'Taganrog', after the main base of the VKS A-50-fleet. Notable is the total of 18 mission markings applied in the form of red stars below the cockpit. (Artwork by Tom Cooper)

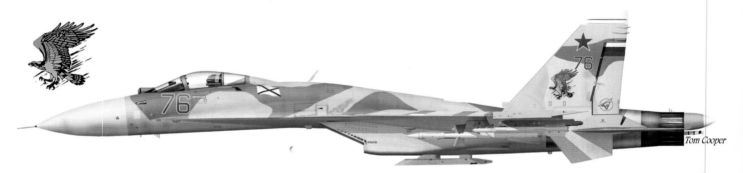

This was one of 15 Su-33s deployed by the 279th Independent Ship-borne Fighter Aviation Regiment on board the aircraft carrier *Kuznetsov* for the cruise to Syria in late 2016. Original colours should have been light grey (FS 25622, on undersurfaces too), blue (FS35250), and dark blue (FS 15012), with radomes and other dielectric panels in traffic white (FS17925), but in most of cases, the camouflage pattern was quite bleached. As usual, the Russian Navy's ensign was applied below the rear part of the cockpit, and the crest of the Sukhoi on the fin. Envisaged as air superiority fighters, the Russian Navy's Su-33s were only equipped with air-to-air missiles (usually a pair each of R-27Rs and R-73s), and up to two 500kg bombs. (Artwork by Tom Cooper)

The Kamov Ka-31 is a little-known airborne early warning variant of the Ka-27, developed to serve as a radar picket for the Russian Navy. Its primary mission system is the NNIIRT/Nizhny Novgorod E-801 Oko pulse-Doppler radar, with a maximum detection range of 110-115km (68-71 miles). The big antenna of the latter is installed under the fuselage, and must be folded before landing. Bort '232' was the second prototype built from scratch at the Kumertau plant in 2006, for tests of the mission system: it was deployed together with another example during Kuznetsov's Mediterranean-cruise in late 2016, and often sighted flying over Lattakia. (Artwork by Tom Cooper)

Syria acquired a total of 55 L-39ZO and 44 L-39ZA armed trainers from Czechoslovakia in the 1970s and 1980s. Both variants boast four underwing hardpoints for light bombs of up to 250 kilograms, or pods for unguided rockets. The L-39ZAs also have a twin-barrel 23-millimetre cannon installed under the fuselage. Around 50 were operational with the Kweres-based 77th Training Brigade and the Advanced Flight School at Ksheesh in 2011. Attrition during the first years of the war was heavy, but about 22-24 L-39s were rushed through overhauls by The Works at Nayrab in 2015-2016 and by 2017 the type remained the principal fighter-bomber of the SyAAF. Meanwhile, all wear a genuine camouflage pattern, consisting of orange-sand and blue-green on top surfaces and sides, and light blue or blue colour on undersurfaces. The principal armament consists of B-8M pods for 80mm unguided rockets, here shown on the L-39ZO serial number 2062. (Artwork by Tom Cooper)

This is a reconstruction of the Su-22M-4 serial number 3224, flown by Major Ali Fahed from No. 677 Squadron, SyAAF, shot down by a USN F/A-18E Super Hornet on 18 June 2017. The aircraft was one of about a dozen locally overhauled examples, and thus painted in a genuine pattern consisting of beige (BS381C/388), dark earth (BS381C/350), and green (similar to FS34098) on upper surfaces and sides, and a dark 'version' of light admiralty grey on undersurfaces. The aircraft is shown as configured during its final mission: with a total of four FAB-250-270 bombs and 1,300-litre drop tanks. (Artwork by Tom Cooper)

The Su-24MK2 serial number 3508 was one of about 16 aircraft still in service with the as-Seen-based No. 696 and Tiyas-based No. 19 Squadrons, as of 2015. Like all Su-24MKs exported in the late 1980s and early 1990s, it was painted in a version of the 'standard' camouflage pattern consisting of dark earth (Russian colour 670 Light Brown, similar to BS381C/350) and dark brown-green (Russian colour 667 Brown, similar to BS381C/641) on top surfaces, and medium blue or German 'hellblau' (similar to FS35526) on sides and undersurfaces. It is shown in typical weapons configuration for this type in SyAAF service, including a total of eight FAB-250M-62 bombs. (Artwork by Tom Cooper)

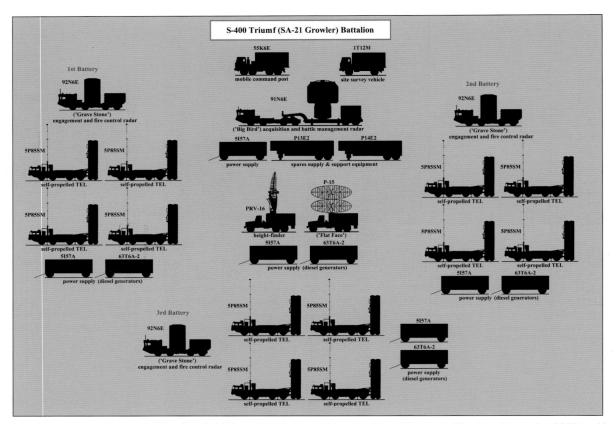

This diagram details the composition of the Russian S-400 battalion deployed for protection of Hmeimim AB, since November 2015, as identified in various photographs and videos. The centrepiece of the unit are the 55K6E mobile command post and the 91N6E acquisition and battle management radar. In place of more advanced early warning radars, older P-15 long-range radar and a PRV-16 height-finder radar were deployed instead – and reinforced by one 39N6E Kasta acquisition radar assigned to the battery of 96K6 Pantsir-S1/S2 SAMs deployed for close-in protection of the Hmeimim AB. Each of the three batteries should be controlled by one 92N6E engagement and fire control radar, but so far only one of these has been identified on different photographs, and this seem to be supporting all 12 5P85SM TELs. (Diagram by Tom Cooper)

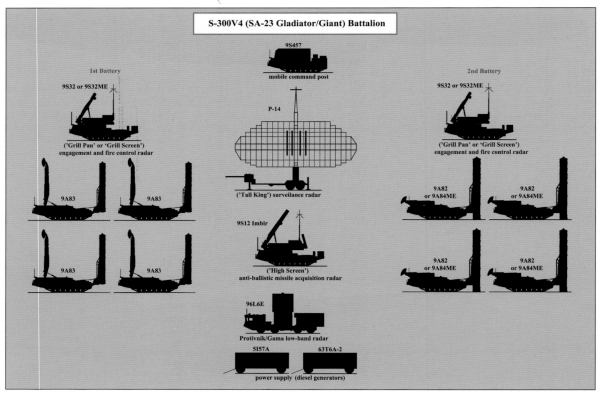

While the possible deployment of the S-300V4 SAM-system to Syria for about eight months in 2016-2017 has never been definitely confirmed, provided this was positioned outside Masyaf, its configuration was approximately as depicted in this diagram. Controlled from the 9S457 mobile command post, this battalion used a SyAAF-operated P-14 long-range, early warning radar, but also its own 9S12 Imbir and 96L6E acquisition radars, while its two or three batteries were served by 9S32 or 9S32ME engagement and fire-control radars, and systems carried by their 9A83 TELARs. Instead of S-300, the Russians have meanwhile deployed another S-400 battalion consisting of three batteries at the same place. (Diagram by Tom Cooper)

causing over 100 casualties (including more than 40 killed). The seriousness of the situation became obvious on 25 March, when even the vaunted Su-35S' and Su-30SMs began flying interdiction strikes along the roads connecting Jishr ash-Shughour, Sarqib and Kfar Zita, armed with little other than B-8M pods for unguided rockets. The SyAAF was meanwhile bombing Khan Sheykhoun, held by the HTS: the town was hit by several OTR-21 Tochka (ASCC-code 'SS-21 Scarab') ballistic missiles, too. Air strikes were further intensified during the following days, peaking at 150 registered take-offs from Hmeimim AB on 3 April.[153]

It was during these operations that the VKS introduced to combat its much improved Su-25SM-3s. Equipped with the SOLT-25 nav/attack suite including a laser/TV/IR sensor and a modern HUD, this variant greatly eased the workload of its pilots, and made it easier for them to strike moving targets. However, because the Su-25SM-3 remained over-dependent on the GLONASS for delivering free-fall bombs, and the accuracy of bombs deployed from higher altitudes remained poor, their pilots began operating at lower altitudes, relying on the Vitebsk-25 active self-protection system for defence against anti-aircraft fire, and MANPADs in particular. Furthermore, the Su-25SM-3s deployed to Syria in early 2017 seemingly lacked the Metronom's rapid targeting capability. Thus, instead of operating in cooperation with the FACs, the upgraded Su-25s were primarily deployed in the mode actually preferred by their pilots: that of the 'free hunt', in which the pilot searches autonomously for targets.[154]

Air strikes on the traffic along the roads connecting Jishr ash-Shughour with Sarqib and Kfar Zita were further intensified over the following days. By that time, the majority of VKS' attacks were flown without the crews knowing what they are going to bomb before their take-off: instead, the primary means of targeting-intelligence became the FACs and the UAVs. Correspondingly, the VKS would launch an entire wave of fighter-bombers, and then let them orbit near probable target areas until they received bombing coordinates. Up to four big waves were launched every day, often comprising up to 40 aircraft. For example, between 1630hrs and 1853hrs on 27 March 2017, the roads between Jishr ash-Shughour and Kfar Zita alone were subjected to attacks of 50 fighter-bombers and 10 helicopters. Even then, other VKS air strikes – and the few still flown by the SyAAF – continued targeting civilian facilities and hospitals in particular. In April 2017 alone, eight medical facilities in Idlib were hit – several of them three or even four times – causing dozens of deaths and injuries among patients and medical personnel. Although it was often impossible to precisely identify the perpetrators, VKS aircraft were clearly recognized as being involved in at least five cases. In turn, for most of April 2017, fighter bombers of both air forces are not known to have flown more than a handful of air strikes against the areas controlled by Daesh.[155]

During the same period, the GRF found itself confronted with multiple attacks on Hmeimim AB, and also facing other kind of threats. Only months later did it become known that the Pantsir-S1/S2 SAM-sites protecting the Russian air base, but also the naval facility in Tartus and the bases in the Masyaf area, had engaged numerous targets, including several shells or artillery rockets, Israeli-operated Heron and Turkish operated Byraktar UAVs, and others, as listed in Table 6.

Table 6: Known Claims by GRF's Pantsir-S1/S2 SAM-Systems, 2017[156]

Date 2017	Area	Target	Target Range (km)	Altitude (km)	Target velocity (km/h)	Number of SAMs fired
23 Mar	Masyaf	balloon	5	2	360	1
27 Mar	Hmeimim	shell/rocket	4	2	1080	1
27 Mar	Hmeimim	shell/rocket	3	1.5	980	1
29 Mar	Hmeimim	shell/rocket	5	4	1320	1
9 Apr	Tartus	Heron UAV	13.7	6.4	120	1
4 May	Masyaf	mini-UAV	3.5	1.5	60	1
11 May	Tartus	Bayraktar UAV	3.2	2.5	110	1
20 May	Tartus	Heron UAV	8.8	7.3	147	1
27 May	Tartus	RQ-21A UAV	5	9.1	110	1
17 Jun	Hmeimim	balloon	15.1	11.7	90	1
21 Jun	Tartus	unclear	19	7,3	100	1
6 Jul	Masyaf	Heron UAV	16.1	4.1	75	1

Despite the presence of this Il-20M – photographed while overflying Idlib on 5 April 2017 – the HQ GRF had failed to recognize preparations for the insurgent and jihadist offensive on Hama. (Photo by Mohammed Owaid)

A Su-34 loaded with at least four – probably six – ODAB-500 thermobaric bombs, thundering down the runway for a take-off on another combat sortie. ODAB-500s were used in huge numbers during the VKS' air strikes on Lataminah and Kfar Zita in April, May and June 2017. (Russian Ministry of Defence)

A still from one of the rare videos released by Moscow during this period, showing a VKS Su-24M (Bort '53 Blue') in the process of taking-off from Hmeimim AB, in May 2017. (Russian Ministry of Defence)

The Ministry of Defence in Moscow has released remarkably little detail about the VKS involvement in the fighting in southern Idlib and northern Hama of March-June 2017. This Su-34 was photographed while returning to Hmeimim AB in September of the same year. Note the absence of air-to-air missiles: instead, the aircraft was equipped with hardpoints for the carriage of up to 10 bombs of up to 500kg. (Russian Ministry of Defence)

During their offensive on Hama, launched in March 2017, Syrian insurgents found themselves out of position to do any more than sporadically harass Hmeimim AB with single artillery rockets. Nevertheless, they regularly plastered the Hama AB (used by the SyAAF only) with BM-21 rockets, sometimes disturbing flying operations for hours, other times for days. (FSyA release)

Chemical Attack on Khan Sheykhoun

Confronted with ever heavier counterattacks of the Axis forces, sustained Russian air strikes on its supply infrastructure, and lack of cooperation on the part of the HTS, the FSyA units were eventually forced to withdraw into defence lines between Halfaya and Souran, and then into the heavily fortified Lataminah Salient, by the end of March 2017. Nevertheless, the HTS continued attacking Qamahana, regularly deploying SVBIEDs that caused heavy casualties to the local militias. Thus, and in reaction to rumours that several jihadist leaders would be meeting in Khan Sheykhoun, at 0630hrs on the morning of 4 April, the Su-22M-4 flown by the Colonel Yusuf Hasouri, deputy commander 'Ba'ath Squadron 677' from Shayrat, dropped two bombs filled with Sarin on that town. At least 110 civilians, including dozens of children, were murdered within minutes. Three hours later, as the rescue services were still busy evacuating about 600 injured, a single Su-24MK2 from T.4 bombed the MSF-supported hospital outside the town, too.[157]

Basing his decision on the UN Security Council's Resolution 2118, the new President of the USA, Donald Trump, ordered the US military into retaliatry strikes. In the pre-dawn hours of 7 April 2017, the destroyers USS *Ross* (DDG-71) and USS *Porter* (DDG-78) underway south of Crete fired a total of 59 BGM-109 Tomahawk Land Attack Missiles (TLAMs) on Shayrat AB. While one of the missiles malfunctioned and crashed outside Tartus, the other 58 hit a total of 44 different objects on the Syrian air base, including numerous hardened aircraft shelters, 10 ammunition depots, 7 workshops, 7 fuel depots, and some of the weapons of the SA-6-equipped 136th Air Defence Brigade responsible for protecting this facility. Foremost, the Tomahawks wrecked at least 12, probably up to 15 fighter-bombers parked inside or in front of various hardened aircraft shelters.[158]

Instantly downplayed by the Kremlin-controlled media in particular, the TLAM-strike on Shayrat had broken the back of

The destruction of at least a dozen MiG-23MLs (like this example, serial number 2771, from 'Ba'ath Squadron 678' photographed inside a hardened aircraft shelter at Hamma AB, in November 2015) and Su-22s at Shayrat AB, on 7 April 2017, broke the back of what was left of the SyAAF. (Syrian Ministry of Defence)

the SyAAF. Before this attack, this base was launching 10 combat sorties a day on average; ever since, this figure dropped to less than a handful. Indeed, ever since, the entire SyAAF has proven unable to fly more than about 36 combat sorties per day – including those by helicopters. This figure decreased further after Jaysh an-Nasir blasted the Hama AB with a volley of BM-21s, destroying at least four operational aircraft and helicopters, on 16 April. The VKS did its best to replace its allies by flying a record-breaking 155 registered sorties from Hmeimim AB on each of 16 and 17 April 2017. The principal targets became the towns of Kfar Zita and Lataminah, both of which were repeatedly plastered by ODAB-500s – although the Russians had been well aware for years that the effectiveness of thermobaric bombs was greatly diminished by the relatively high position of this area above sea level.[159]

Nevertheless, this Russian aerial offensive – which continued until the early June of 2017 – was to prove the third crucial military operation in this war. It not only mauled the HTS, virtually neutralising its capability to run large-scale offensive operations, but it caused sufficient damage to the insurgent and jihadist supply infrastructure in Idlib that it became obvious – apparently in Ankara and in Doha, too – that any further offensive operations would be pointless without a major escalation of hostilities against Russia (for example through provision of serious air defences). This was a step none of the foreign powers was ready to take. After

this defeat, the Syrian insurgency and the JAN failed to launch any further offensive operations. In turn, this freed thousands of Axis troops for operations against isolated or besieged insurgent-controlled pockets in central and southern Syria. As time was to show, the fate of the same was thus sealed, once and forever.

The remaining fleet of SyAAF's Su-22s was more than halved by the TLAM strike on Shayrat AB. Ever since, this air force has struggled to fly even 50 percent of the combat sorties it used to fly before 7 April 2017. This example – serial 3235 – was one of four survivors of the US attack. (Syrian Ministry of Defence)

The US TLAM-strike on Shayrat AB has once again exposed the vulnerability of the Russian air defences in Syria. Correspondingly, since summer of 2017, the VKS has regularly deployed Beriev A-50U airborne early warning aircraft to Hmeimim AB. Visible on this photograph are Borts 37 ('Sergey Atayants', RF-93966, background) and Bort 41 ('Taganrog', RF-94268, foreground). (Russian Ministry of Defence)

CHAPTER 6
RUSSIAN DOMINANCE

The first sign of a reinforced Russian position in Syria became obvious through the establishment of the 30th Division RGD and the V Corps, in November 2016, at the height of the final battle for Aleppo. Due to the chronic lack of troops loyal to the Assad government, related recruiting, reorganisation and re-training of diverse militias came forward rather slowly, early on. The situation experienced a dramatic change following the loss of Palmyra and then the rumours about the supposed coup attempt by Maher and the IRGC in late January 2017. During the following few weeks, reports surfaced about the units of the 4th Division receiving orders to deploy well away from Damascus,

while Russian advisors intensified the reorganisation of various militias into the RGD and the SAA. Always neatly corseted by the Tiger Force, the resulting formations were further reinforced through the deployment of the Russian PMC Wagner, and elements of the Russian Army, including FACs. From Moscow's point of view, the affairs in Syria thus finally began turning in the desired direction: the position of Russian-supported Bashar al-Assad vis-à-vis the IRGC-QF-supported Maher was significantly bolstered, and GRF's officers had established themselves as the party in Damascus that had the final say with regards to almost all the combat operations.[160]

The Wild East

The resulting mix of reconstituted SAA units, controlled by the Tiger Force and commanded by Russian officers – the V Corps – was put to its first test in late February and early March 2017, during an offensive against Daesh in Palmyra. Well-supported by Russian FACs, VKS' Su-25s and attack helicopters, and by L-39s and Su-22s, this operation proved a success, and the – meanwhile largely ruined and looted – town was finally liberated from the extremists on 2 March 2017.

Emboldened, and in the light of negotiations between Moscow, Ankara, and Tehran (the result of which was the decision to create four 'de-escalation zones', including the Idlib province, the insurgent-controlled RTP and Eastern Ghouta, and most of the Dera'a province), Axis forces next launched an offensive against FSyA units in south-eastern Syria in May 2017. Supported by the 9th Battalion of the 31st Airborne Brigade of the Russian Army, they advanced from Suwayda towards the border of Iraq – obviously with the intention of establishing a land connection to IRGC-Q proxies in the latter country. Lacking in cover and fire-power, the insurgent units withdrew into a perimeter of about 30 kilometres around their US-run training camps in the Tanf area. However, when the Iranian-controlled part of the involved forces attempted to attack this perimeter, the US CENTCOM issued a warning: when this was ignored, US aircraft bombed the IRGC-QF's proxies, destroying four MBTs, a ZSU-23-4, and several other vehicles on 15 May 2017. After reorganizing, the Axis forces attempted a new attack from the south on 8 June 2017. Although US combat aircraft had forced two Su-22s of the SyAAF to turn away, and shot down an IRGC-QF-operated Shahed-129 armed UAV, on the same day, 24 hours later the Axis forces reached the border about 30 kilometres north of Tanf – thus establishing the land corridor to Iran (via Iraq) which Tehran had sought for years.[161]

Further north, Axis forces attempted to reach Tabqa and then Raqqa on the Euphrates River before the US-supported

Combatants of the IRGC-QF's Kata'ib Imam Ali in the Tanf area in June 2017. (IRGC release)

A T-72 operated by one of the IRGC-QF-controlled units in eastern Syria in summer 2017. (IRGC release)

PKK/PYD/YPG/SDF-conglomerate could do so. This attempt misfired, not only because of an airborne assault, supported by US air-power, that quickly secured Tabqa, but also due to a fierce defence by Daesh, and then a series of minor clashes in the Jardin area, further south. The worst of this occurred on 18 June 2017, when one of five Su-22s launched from Shayrat and Tiyas approached the area around the village of JaDen, following a few minor clashes on the ground. Alarmed by the fact that the SyAAF pilot was ignoring their requests to turn away while approaching the positions of the US-supported forces, the lead of four F/A-18 Hornets of the US Navy present on the scene eventually decided to open fire. At 1843hrs, he fired one AIM-9X from a range of 600 metres, then – without waiting for results – an AIM-120C. One of the missiles blotted the Sukhoi out of the sky, forcing the pilot, Major Ali Fahed from No. 677 Squadron, to eject.[162]

The Central Syria Campaign

Undeterred, the Axis forces continued manoeuvring further east and south, and on 14 July 2017 launched the so-called Central Syria Campaign, with the aim of lifting the siege of Dayr az-Zawr. Initially run in the form of a myriad of diverse militias and PMCs storming the oil and gas-rich central Syria from multiple directions, this effort resulted in several large groups of Daesh being encircled in villages of eastern Hama and Homs provinces as of mid-August. Despite multiple counterattacks by the extremists, Axis forces continued pushing and, on 27 August, launched their advance from Sukhna on Dayr az-Zawr. Supported by heavy air strikes by SyAAF's L-39s and VKS' Su-25s and attack helicopters, they finally established contact with the northern pocket on 5 September 2017. Two days later, the siege of the air base, further south, was broken too.[163]

Ever since, it has primarily been the IRGC-QF that has run operations against remaining gangs of Daesh in this part of Syria. As far as is known, time and again these have received significant Russian support. In addition to four Su-25s and a similar number of combat helicopters meanwhile deployed at Dayr az-Zawr AB, the offensive on al-Bukamal – opened on 31 October 2017, and including the Hezbollah/Lebanon, Liwa Fatemiyoun, Harakat Hezbollah an-Nujba (a new name for the merger of the former Kata'ib Hezbollah and Harakat an-Nujba), and Liwa al-Qods – received fire-support in the form of six Kalibr cruise missiles fired from the attack submarine *Nizhny Novgorod*, underway in the Mediterranean. On the same day, six Tu-22M-3 bombers attacked six different targets outside the town.[164] Two days later, Tu-22M-3s flew another series of air strikes on the al-Bukamal area, which was also subsequently hit by six Kalibr cruise missiles fired by the attack submarine *Kolpino*. Additional Tu-22M-3 attacks were flown on 3 November: with one exception (an area about 28 kilometres north of al-Bukamal), the precise targets of the air strikes and cruise missile attacks, and also of several surface-to-surface missiles fired by Axis forces – remain unknown.[165]

The IRGC-QF's advance reached the outskirts of al-Bukamal on 9 November 2017. However, related reports of victory – which caused a sort of euphoria in Moscow – proved premature. Daesh seemed to have let Iranian-commanded troops into the town, only to launch a stunning counterattack the following night: as well as killing at least 30 Iranian-commanded troops, this prompted the survivors to flee in panic. Furthermore, three days later the extremists launched a suicide attack on Dayr az-Zawr AB, where three L-39s were destroyed on the ground, and claimed a VKS helicopter as shot down near al-Ward Nord oilfield, in the Salihiyah area. As 'retaliation', Moscow ordered additional air strikes by Tu-22M-3s, and these bombed multiple villages around al-Bukamal in the following days, although it was well-known that these were primarily full of civilian refugees. Axis forces managed to secure al-Bukamal only after their large-scale reorganisation and a pincer-attack on 18 November 2017. Even then, and although the town was declared as the 'last bastion' of Daesh in Syria, fighting in this part of the country is still on-going at the time of writing.

Attack submarine *Kolpino* re-loading Kalibr missiles off the coast of Syria in November 2017. (Russian Ministry of Defence)

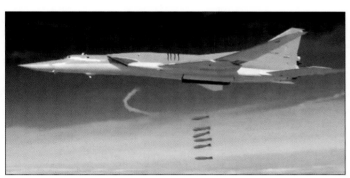

A Tu-22M-3 (Bort '57 Red', RF-34079) releasing six FAB-500M-62 bombs over eastern Syria in November 2017. (Russian Ministry of Defence)

A Su-25SM of the VKS underway low over eastern Syria, while carrying four B-8M pods for S-8K 80mm unguided rockets. Shortly after the siege of Dayr az-Zawr Four was lifted, up to four such fighter-bombers were deployed to the local air base. (Syrian social media)

This group of trucks reportedly carried the forward HQ of the Russian Army detachment to the V Corps during the advance on Dayr az-Zawr in summer 2017. The troops in question continued supporting the Axis forces at least until the IRGC-QF's advance on al-Bukamal in November of the same year. (IRGC release)

Another of the Tu-22M-3s involved in combat operations in support of the IRGC-QF's offensive on al-Bukamal was this example, Bort '42 Red' (RF-94142). Note the application of a total of 23 'mission markings' (in the form of red stars), in front of the left side of the cockpit: according to unconfirmed reports, each stands for 10 combat sorties. (Russian Ministry of Defence)

The Mess in Idlib

Meanwhile, during September 2017 the VKS had increased the number of Su-34s at Hmeimim AB to 12, and even deployed three MiG-29SMTs to Syria.[166] Despite agreements with Iran and Turkey, and despite impressions created by continuous misreporting from Moscow, and just as over the last two years, the reinforced Aviation Group continued bombing the insurgent and HTS-controlled Idlib and western Aleppo. Unsurprisingly, the Daesh surrounded in eastern Hama then exploited the opportunity to break out in a western direction and attack the HTS on 9 October 2017. As the fighting continued, the Axis commanders exploited the opportunity and launched an attack from the direction of Ithriya, with the intention of reaching Abu ad-Duhor AB. Supported by more than 350 air strikes, primarily by VKS, flown during the first five days of this operation, but especially by Daesh's attacks on the HTS, they made

Underside view of one of three MiG-29SMTs deployed by the VKS in Syria during the second half of 2017. (Russian Ministry of Defence)

good advance early on, reaching Rahjan by 28 October. Five days later, on 2 November, the Axis forces launched an assault from the north and captured the HTS stronghold of Rashadiyah in the southern Aleppo province, while on 3 November, the RGD-controlled forces captured Shukasiyah in the south – although suffering heavy losses to the TOW-gunners of the Central Division FSyA. The fighting went back and forth for most of the same month, with the Axis and Daesh attacking the HTS, and the latter counter-attacking at every opportunity until the Axis forces managed to circumvent the HTS-held fortified village of Balil on 3 December 2017, while the FSyA forces managed to push Daesh out of southern Idlib a week later.[167]

Third Russian 'Withdrawal'

In the middle of the resulting mess in Idlib, and while the IRGC-QF was fighting bitter battles against Daesh south of Dayr az-Zawr, on 6 December 2017 the Putin government suddenly announced that Syria had been 'completely liberated' of the extremists. Correspondingly, the President of the Russian Federation paid an unannounced visit to Hmeimim AB, five days later, to declare an end to the war and the start of (yet another) withdrawal of Russian troops from the country. During his stay at Hmeimim, Putin met not only Bashar al-Assad but also Brigadier-General Suhail al-Hassan, commander of the 'Tiger Force' – who was awarded one of Russia's highest military decorations, four months earlier. Ever since, al-Hassan – who grew immensely popular amongst supporters of the Assad government – has appeared in public accompanied by Russian special forces personnel, who appear to have been assigned to his close protection. As usual, most of Putin's statements were relativised during the following days. Indeed, by the end of the month, Shoygu has announced the MOD plans to 'form a permanent grouping' of forces 'at the Tartus naval facility and Hmeimim air base'. Thus, nothing has changed: the fighting went on and the VKS continued flying air strikes – primarily against the Syrian opposition.[168]

Meanwhile, the Axis forces in eastern Idlib had regrouped and, after receiving more and better close air support from the VKS than ever before, launched their final push on Abu ad-Duhor on 19 December 2017. It was around this time that HTS received a small batch of 9K38 Strela (ASCC-code 'SA-18 Grouse') MANPADs: one of these was used to shoot down a SyAAF L-39, on 26 December. The pilot – Captain Bassam Hassan – ejected safely, but was captured by the HTS and later executed. Finding no other ways to counter the relentless flow of Russian air strikes, the insurgents infiltrated a mortar team behind enemy lines: on 31 December, this managed to reach the Hmeimim AB and took it under fire. Two Russian military personnel were killed and several aircraft slightly damaged. Two days later, a much more sophisticated attempt was launched in the form of an attack by a total of 13 home-made UAVs, armed with bomblets: 10 of these reportedly went for Hmeimim AB, three for the Russian naval facility in Tartus. This time, the VKS claimed its air defences to have shot down all the vehicles before they could reach their target. Moscow exploited these two attacks to declare its support for the offensive into eastern Idlib – supposedly with the intention of 'pushing terrorists away from its major base' – and to reinforce its bombardment of that area, despite the presence of Turkish military observation posts, meanwhile established to monitor the 'cease-fire'.[169]

Successfully concluded with the recapture of the Abu ad-Duhor AB on 8 January 2018, the Axis offensive against the HTS in eastern Aleppo caused at least 60,000 civilians to flee in the direction of the Turkish border. This massive movement was repeatedly rocketed and bombed by the VKS: especially Su-25-pilots began excelling at targeting trucks, full of civilians, with unguided rockets. The insurgency reacted by grouping technicals, carrying heavy machine guns and light anti-aircraft guns, for the defence of the most frequently attacked points along the roads. On 1 February 2018, VKS' Su-25s heavily bombed Lataminah, Kfar Zita, and Khan Sheykhoun, where one of them was hit by

A Su-25SM (Bort '22 Red') loaded with four ODAB-250-270 bombs taking off for an attack on insurgent-controlled parts of Idlib in late 2017. (Russian Ministry of Defence)

ground fire: apparently, the aircraft in question returned safely to Hmeimim AB. Two days later, the Su-25SM flown by Major Roman Filipov was hit too: this time one of engines caught fire, forcing the pilot to eject. The HTS promptly claimed the kill for itself, and released a video indicating the firing of a single 9K38 Strela for that purpose – and this version of events is generally accepted as genuine. However, the Sukhoi was felled over Ma'asaran, about 10 kilometres north-east of Ma'arat an-Nauman and 2-3 kilometres outside Sarqib: this village was controlled by insurgents of Jaysh an-Nasr and Faylaq ash-Sham and thus outside the reach of HTS and its MANPADs. Convinced he was about to be captured by 'jihadists', upon landing by parachute, Filipov committed suicide with a hand-grenade. His body was returned to Russia via Turkey, just two days later.[170] In an exercise of driving the official agenda ab absurdum, Colonel-General Sergey Surovikin, commander-in-chief of the GRF, subsequently stated that Filipov was, 'flying over the Idlib de-escalation zone for controlling cease-fire regime observance'.[171]

Wreckage of Filipov's Su-25SM (Bort '06 Blue', RF-95486) as found by local insurgents. (Jaysh an-Nasr release)

Osas of Eastern Ghouta

Once the IRGC-QF had 'stabilised' the situation in Idlib, and brought most of eastern Syria under its control, the Assad government became eager to destroy the remaining insurgent-controlled enclaves in the suburbs of Damascus and Eastern Ghouta in early 2018. Under constant siege and daily air strikes for five years, the northern part of the area in question was controlled by the Saudi Arabian-supported Jaysh al-Islam (JAI), while its southern sections were under the control of the Faylaq ar-Rahman, the HTS, and a few other factions. From the standpoint of aerial warfare, note that Eastern Ghouta used to have very potent air defences: defectors from the SAA and the SyAAF brought with them a large number of light anti-aircraft guns, and, in early October 2012, the JAI had overrun a SAM-site west of Maydaa, where it captured five BAZ-5937 transporter-erector-launcher (TEL) vehicles for the 9K33M2 Osa-AK system (ASCC-code 'SA-8 Gecko'), and 12 related 9M33M2 missiles. Theoretically, operating a SAM-system with a radar range of 20 kilometres, and a missile range of 15 kilometres, a combination of

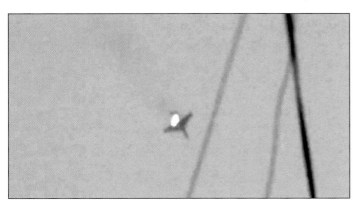

Dramatic still from a video showing Filipov's Su-25SM falling towards the ground, with at least one (left) engine afire. (HTS release)

just three or four operational SA-8 vehicles would have been enough to seal the skies over Eastern Ghouta. However, this never happened: instead, the JAI put its Osa-AKs into action only sporadically: between 2013 and 2015, they scored about half a dozen kills, the most spectacular of which included the downing of a SyAAF Su-24MK2 on 11 June 2015.[172] The reason was not the lack of trained personnel or any action from the SyAAF or other of forces of the Assad regime: although in possession of such Soviet-made anti-radar missiles as the Kh-28 (ASCC-code 'AS-9 Kyle'), and diverse guided bombs, the SyAAF proved entirely unable to tackle the emerging threat. Furthermore, although very large vehicles (more than nine metres long and weighting over 17 tonnes when fully loaded), the TELs were carefully hidden. The actual problem was that most of the captured launchers quickly fell in disrepair because of their poor condition, and a little-known weak-spot of this system. The HF-generator of the BAZ-5937 has an average life of only 700 working hours under ideal circumstances, and is based on hopelessly obsolete technology, spares for which are scarce even on the black market.[173]

One of the 9K33M2 Osa-AK TELs captured by the JAI in October 2012. Several of these saw sporadic service until mid-2016, but were out of service by the time of the Axis onslaught on Eastern Ghouta in February 2018. (JAI release)

Contrary to the SyAAF, the VKS did try to find and destroy the captured SAMs: quite soon after the Russian fighter-bombers began bombing this part of Syria, on 15 October 2015, the MOD in Moscow claimed a VKS Su-34 to have knocked out one of JAI's Osas using a KAB-500 PGM. A day or two later, the Jaysh al-Islam appears to have returned the favour by firing one of the Iranian-made Zelzal ballistic missiles it has captured from the IRGC-QF earlier: reportedly, this missed Hmeimim AB by less than 12 kilometres.[174]

In mid-2016, the JAI managed to smuggle enough spares and missiles to Eastern Ghouta to reactivate at least one of the TELARs, and claim several kills against SyAAF aircraft and helicopters. However, subsequently, all the vehicles fell into disrepair and were never deployed in action again. The VKS thus never confronted serious air defences in Syria.

Burning Douma

In the preparation of the offensive on Eastern Ghouta in early 2018, the VKS is known to have reinforced its assets at Hmeimim AB once again: on 20 and 21 February, four Su-35s, four Su-25SMs, and one A-50U SRDLO were deployed to Syria. Indeed, the MOD even permitted the deployment of two prototypes of the Su-57 stealth fighter. Intended to be run in secrecy – amongst other reasons because both aircraft were still lacking most of their avionics suite, had no operational weapons systems, and are not known to have fired or released any weapons in Russia

by that date – this effort was revealed in public only when locals photographed two Su-57s on finals to Hmeimim AB. In turn, this sparked another round of controversial reactions from Moscow, some sources stressing the aircraft were deployed to Syria to test radar and electronic warfare systems, but not to be engaged in active combat. Eventually, both aircraft were flown back to Russia about a week later.[175]

Meanwhile, the VKS offensive on Eastern Ghouta went on in the usual fashion, including indiscriminate bombardment of residential areas with CBUs filled with incendiaries and other types of sub-munition, and with intentional air strikes on markets, schools, civil defence centres and hospitals in particular. With the civilian defences in this part of Syria being reasonably well-developed, much of the population sought shelter in extensive underground bunkers and tunnels meanwhile constructed by the insurgents. Before long, such facilities were overcrowded with thousands of people. Undertaking everything possible in order to coerce insurgent leaders into a capitulation, the VKS and the SyAAF began searching for and striking precisely such objects. Between 0100hrs and 0200hrs on 20 February 2018, multiple bombs were used to collapse a two-storey building upon a shelter where 41 women and children, and one man, were killed. On 16 March, a civilian area including a marketplace in Kfar Batna was bombed and at least 70 civilians killed and another 200 wounded. Three days later, an air strike hit the former Dar as-Salam School Number 3, in Sarout, in Irbin, used as an underground shelter for women and children, killing at least 17 children, 4 women, and one man. On the evening of 22 March, an air strike using RBK-500s filled with thermite-based incendiary bomblets hit the Abdul Rahman Educational Centre in the ad-Duwar area of Irbin, killing at least 10 women, 13 men, and 15 children – most of these from the same family.[176] Eventually at least 28 health facilities had been attacked – especially in the period between 19 and 21 February, and mostly from the air – and even the transport of victims to such places was rendered impossible due to air strikes. As usual, the MOD in Moscow flatly denied any of the related accusations, including deployment of incendiary ammunition – despite obvious evidence. By March 2018, most medical facilities in Eastern Ghouta were either destroyed, or their function severely disrupted. Realising the Western indifference towards such bestialities, and facing an onslaught of Axis forces on the ground, the JAI opened negotiations with representatives of the GRF. When related talks collapsed, in early April, SyAAF helicopters flew a chemical weapons attack on Douma on 7 April 2018, and continued launching air strikes on residential areas, causing deaths of at least 49 individuals and the injuries of up to 650.[177] After this, there was no holding out: the surviving insurgents promptly reached an agreement for their evacuation, and that of their families – about 50,000 people in total – to Idlib. On 14 April 2018, Damascus announced the capture of the entire pocket, thus achieving one of the biggest victories in this war.

Clashes with the USA

On 18 June 2016, a pair of Su-24s bombed the base of the US-supported New Syrian Army in the Tanf area, near the joint borders between Iraq, Jordan, and Syria. The US CENTCOM promptly diverted a pair of US Navy F/A-18 Hornet fighter-bombers to the scene, and their pilots tried to call the Russians on a previously agreed-upon communications channel, but they did not receive any answers. When the Hornets distanced in order to refuel in the air, a pair of Su-34 came in and hit the same base with several CBUs. Acting as if it didn't know about the US-supported 'New Syrian Army' force deployed along the border between Syria and Jordan, the MOD in Moscow denied the bombing any of US-backed forces, explaining that, 'the object which has suffered bombardment was located more than 300km far from the borders of territories claimed by the American party as ones controlled by the opposition joined the ceasefire regime', and Russian forces 'forewarned members states of the US-led coalition about the ground targets to strike on'.[178]

While this incident remained without repercussions, the few that followed in 2017 created enough tensions for Moscow and Washington to agree a 'deconfliction line' in October of the same year, according to which, the airspace 'east' (i.e. north) of the Euphrates River was under US control, and that south of the river under Russian control. Nevertheless, on 15 November 2017, a pair of Fairchild A-10 Thunderbolt IIs of the USAF nearly collided head on with a Russian Su-24 – east of the Euphrates River. Two days later, two F-22s encountered an armed Su-24 that had crossed into the airspace east of the Euphrates, and made three passes directly over allied ground forces: the VKS crew failed to react to five attempts by US pilots to establish radio contact. On 13 December 2017, two F-22 Raptors intercepted two Su-25s underway inside the airspace considered as 'US controlled': when US pilots attempted to warn the Russians away, one of the Su-25s flew so close to one F-22 that it the latter had to aggressively manoeuvre to avoid a collision.[179] As usual, the MOD in Moscow denied such reports, claiming that a pair of Su-25 that 'escorted a humanitarian convoy near Mayadin', west of the Euphrates, was approached by one F-22 that released decoy flares while remaining on the east side, in this fashion, 'interfering with the flight path' of the Russian aircraft. Correspondingly, a Su-35 then approached the F-22 from the rear and forced it to leave the area.[180]

A much more serious incident took place in the Dayr az-Zawr area in early February 2018, resulting in what was often misdescribed as a 'direct clash' between the US and Russian militaries. According to unofficial reports from Damascus, the Assad government had been secretly negotiating with the US-supported PKK/PYD/YPG/SDF-conglomerate about a take-over of the so-called Conoco oilfield (known as 'Tabiye' in Damascus), a few kilometres east of Dayr az-Zawr, since October 2017. A related agreement was reached in early February, and thus a combined Axis force attempted to move in.[181]

As usual, the force in question was a hodgepodge of IRGC-QF-controlled militias, nominally run by the 4th Division. Most of them were made up from three of battalions the IRGC and 4th Division-linked Liwa al-Baqir recently established in the villages of Mazlum, Marrat and al-Hatlah (all on the eastern bank of Euphrates). Staffed by tribesmen of Bekara and Albo Hamad tribes, these units were granted US-permission to be stationed on the eastern bank of the Euphrates under condition that their number remained limited to 400. The Liwa al-Bakr then established a base in the village of Tabiya, where it received support from about 20 mercenaries of the (Russian) Wagner PMC.

Informed by their Iranian commanders that they would be fighting a 'Daesh sleeper cell', the combatants of the Liwa Fatemiyoun and the 4th Division had crossed the Euphrates River at 0500hrs local time on the morning of 7 February 2018, before moving south. At 2200hrs the same day, they approached the positions of the PKK/YPD/YPG/SDF in the village of Khusham. Because either US or other Western military personnel deployed in Khusham felt threatened by this move, the American reaction was vicious, to put it mildly: after communicating with the HQ GRF in order to ascertain that no Russian military troops were involved, the Central Command of the US military unleashed a series of air strikes by F-15E Strike Eagle, F-22 Raptors, and Lockheed Martin AC-130J gunships of the USAF, and Boeing AH-64 Apache helicopter gunships of the US Army. The air strikes were further intensified when CENTCOM identified a second force moving out of the base in Tabiya: this was subjected to a series of particularly devastating blows, reinforced by the artillery of the US Marine Corps units deployed further north. According to various sources, three hours of US attacks left more than 200 of the attackers dead, including 80 combatants from the 4th Division, around 100 Iraqis and Afghans from the Liwa Fatemiyoun, and around 70 tribal fighters from the Liwa al-Bakr. One PKK/PYD/YPD/SDF's spokespersons later claimed the destruction of more than 20 vehicles, including 9 'tanks'.[182]

While much of the international media subsequently exaggerated its reporting about the extent of the Russian involvement in this operation, and especially about 'massive' Russian casualties, the Wagner PMC actually lost only about a dozen mercenaries deployed in Tabiya: they had the bad luck of being in the wrong place at the wrong time. Always cautious to avoid a direct military confrontation – and with relations between the Putin government and the Russian mercenaries in Syria being 'tense' at least – Moscow and Washington officials thus went to quite some lengths to either avoid commenting, or to downplay the entire affair. Indeed, another similar incident was (narrowly) avoided about a month later.[183]

IRGC's Mini-War with Israel

At around 0400hrs local time on 10 February 2018, the IRGC-QF unit deployed at Tiyas AB launched a stealthy Saeqeh UAV. Approximately 20 minutes later, and after 'cutting the corner' through Jordanian airspace, the propeller-driven aircraft entered Israeli airspace. At 0425hrs, a Boeing AH-64 Apache helicopter from No. 113 Squadron, Israeli Air & Space Force (IASF), intercepted the UAV and shot it down near Beit Shehan, in north-eastern Israel. The IASF reacted within 30 minutes: around 0500hrs in the morning, it scrambled at least eight, probably more, of its Lockheed-Martin F-16Is, and several formations of Boeing F-15Is into an attack on several 'Iranian targets' in Syria, foremost in the area around the Tiyas AB. The fighter-bombers appear to have flown in two directions: one continuing over Lebanon, the other first passing through Jordanian airspace before turning in a north-eastern direction. Around 0530hrs, the Israelis began releasing a number of stand-off PGMs, including numerous Delilahs, GBU-39 and GBU-53 small-diameter bombs. As far as is known, these demolished much of Tiyas AB, including its control tower, the IRGC-QF's mobile control station for UAVs, several unmanned aircraft, and numerous support buildings. The air base was 'out of commision' for days afterwards. Mere minutes later, dozens of reports in the Lebanese and Syrian social media indicated quite a vicious response from the SyAAF's air defences against aircraft underway over northern and southern Lebanon. These included the firing of at least eight SAMs, including several V-880s (missile of the S-200VM Vega system, code-named 'SA-5 Gammon' by the ASCC/NATO) by the main SAM-site of the 16th Air Defence Regiment, positioned about 20 kilometres east of Dmeyr AB. Minutes before 0600hrs, an Israeli F-16I fighter-bomber erupted in flames and then crashed about 10 kilometres east of Haifa, in northern Israel.[184]

Official Israeli statements subsequently blamed the crew of the downed F-16I for being preoccupied with attempts to verify that its PGMs had hit selected targets, and thus exposing their aircraft to enemy air defences for much too long: although the fighter-bomber was certainly streaming its Israeli Aerial Towed Decoy, this enabled one of the SAMs fired at it to proximity fuse closely enough to cause fatal damage. When the jet went out of control, the crew was left without option but to eject: the pilot suffered 'moderate' injuries', while the weapons system officer landed safely.[185]

After encountering such a barrage of SAMs, the IASF launched the second wave of fighter-bombers into attacks on selected targets north, west, south-west and south-east of Damascus. Around 0845hrs, the first of several PGMs hit Dmeyr AB, and the positions of the 16th Air Defence Regiment. Almost simultaneously, the HQ of the 4th Division in the Madaya area was demolished by several guided bombs, as was the local IRGC-QF HQ and the Ba'ath Party HQ in ad-Dimas. A few kilometres further west, the HQ of the 104th Brigade RGD, and positions of an unknown air defence regiment in ad-Reige received multiple hits. The Israelis then targeted the IRGC-QF HQ in Tal Abu at-Tha'leb (or 'Abu Thalib'), the HQ of the 1st Division SAA (meanwhile housing another IRGC-base) and positions of the 165th Air Defence Regiment, SyAAF, in the Kisweh area. By 0900hrs, the IASF also hit four air defence sites in the Dera'a area, including the 89th Air Defence Regiment (SyAAF) outside the villae of Jubab, the 79th Air Defence Regiment outside Sanamen, the 157th Air Defence Regiment outside Tel as-Sebbah (targeted by a total of '18 winged

Saeqeh UAVs, of the same type as the one the IRGC-QF sent into Israeli airspace on the morning of 10 February 2018. (IRGC release)

missiles', that destroyed the command post, killing two), and the 175th Air Defence Regiment outside Izra, near the Khekhlekh AB. This time, the SyAAF reacted by firing up to 20 SAMs, including numerous SA-5s, SA-6s and SA-11s: none of these scored any hits, but several ended their flights in south-eastern Lebanon and northern Jordan. The exact number of casualties on the Iranian and Syrian side remains unknown, but one of those killed was Major-General Ahmed Mohammed Hosseinou, Chief-of-Staff of the Department of Chemical Protection – the de-facto 'Chemical Ali' of Syria. Furthermore, Harakat Hezbollah an-Nujba subsequently published the name of at least one of its commanders killed by Israeli air strikes.

A still from a video released by the IDF, showing two hangars in north-western corner of the Tiyas AB, together with an IRGC-QF-operated UAV (probably Mohajer-4) – shortly before the IASF's counterattack on the morning of 10 February 2018. (IDF release)

Moment of Truth

Despite Putin's announcement that the war was over, and massive successes of Axis force in the south of the country, the war in Syria actually continued – and Russian military forces remained intensively involved. While the MOD in Moscow had released few related statements since December 2017, this fact became obvious on 7 May 2018, when a Ka-52 of the VKS was shot down by Daesh over eastern Syria, killing the crew – including the pilot, Lieutenant-Colonel Nikolay Gushchin, and navigator/gunner Lieutenant Roman Miroshnichenko.

Similarly, despite the succesfull destruction of the insurgent-controlled Eastern Ghouta, in April 2018, followed by a similar operation that overran the insurgent-controled parts of Dera'a, in June and July of the same year – with which all of southern and central Syria was under the nominal control of the Assad government for the first time since 2011 – most of the Idlib province and north-eastern Lattakia remain under the control of Turkish-supported Syrian insurgents, while most of northern Syria remains under the control of the US-supported PKK/PYD/YPG/SDF-conglomerate. At the time this book is going to press, in August 2018, the Assad government was running negotiations with the latter, while launching bombastic announcements about a coming offensive on Idlib.

Meanwhile, the Israeli-Iranian clashes have fully exposed the massive presence of the IRGC-QF and its proxies in Syria. Certainly enough, officials in Damascus and Moscow reacted by attempting to create the impression of operations in the Damascus and Dera'a areas being run exclusively by the RGD, the V Corps and the Tiger Force. Moscow refuted all allegations of use of chemical weapons, calling them a fabrication and provocation to justify foreign military action. However, following week-long consultations, the USA, Great Britain and France then launched cruise-missile attacks on the Barzeh Research and Development Centre near Damascus, and Him Shinshar military installations near Homs, on 14 April 2018.

What is surprising for many foreign observers is that – just like the TLAM-strike on Shayrat, a year earlier, and Israeli air strikes on Axis forces in Syria on 10 May 2018 – this action prompted no Russian military reaction. This was not without reason: probably calculating that a greater presence of the IRGC-QF and Hezbollah closer to the cease-fire lines to Israel would increase the risk of further Israeli military actions – to the detriment of the Assad government, in turn undermining Russian interests – Moscow sought to decrease tensions. In May 2018, officers of the GRF have instrumented the disbandment of the Liwa Suqour al-Qunaitra, one of most powerful IRGC-QF-supported militias in south-western Syria, and its merger into the reconstituted 7th Infantry Division, SAA. Obviously unwilling to outright challenge or defy the Russian position, and not keen to trigger a full-scale war with Israel, Tehran accepted such measures. On 23 May, Iran's ambassador to Jordan announced that although Iran maintained its political support for the Assad government, it would not play a role in any potential government offensive in Dera'a province, while five days later Russian Foreign Minister Lavrov stated that only Syrian forces should be present near the country's southern border. Ever since, a host of militias originally established by the IRGC-QF as a part of the NDF, but even some of those originating from Iraq, have stressed their 'Syrian' nature, and declared themselves part of the Syrian armed forces. Nevertheless, when questioned about its ability to effect an Iranian withdrawal from Syria, even official Moscow was forced to admit – several times – that such ideas are 'entirely unrealistic'. Through its military intervention in Syria, the government of Vladimir Putin has thus put Russia into an awkward situation: on one hand, it is responsible for maintaining the Assad government in power; on the other, and because Moscow is neither interested nor in position to bolster the finances of Damascus, the survival of Bashar al-Assad remains heavily dependent on the presence of the IRGC-QF and dozens of thousands of combatants that the same controls, the presence of which riles Israel to the point where its counterattacks threaten the survival of the Assad government.[186]

Russian Air Defences in Syria

Another reason for the Russian reluctance with regards to US and allied, but especially to Israeli, attacks on the IRGC-QF and its proxies in Syria, is the actual vulnerability and isolation of the GRF's position. Already after the US attack on Shayrat, the Putin government and the MOD found themselves facing questions like why the SAM-sites protecting the main GRF bases in Syria failed to counter this attack. Rather amazingly, but in the best traditions of the local style of studying experiences of this kind around the World for the last 70 years, even independent military experts in Russia have failed to provide a satisfactory answer. Certainly enough, some have explained that, while optimised for long-range engagements, the S-400 system at Hmeimim could not detect and engage low-flying cruise missiles targeting Shayrat, because this is over 200 kilometres away – due to the curvature of the Earth's surface. When it transpired that the Russian SAM-sites protecting the port of Tartus failed to intercept the TLAMs, the explanation was that, due to Earth's curvature, systems like S-300 with a maximum range of 100 kilometres, can engage low-flying targets only out to 24-26 kilometres. Another explanation was that the Tomahawks were supported by Boeing F/A-18G Growler aircraft for electronic warfare, and fired within such a short period of time that they passed the Syrian coast close to Tartus de-facto flying in a formation.[187]

However, as evident from the site of one missile that crashed, the 59 TLAMS passed through the Homs gap on their way to Shayrat: as obvious from any map of Syria, and while about 70 kilometres south of Hmeimim, this area is well within 20 kilometres south of Tartus. Thus, the conclusion on hand is that although the US missiles passed 'right under the nose' of the Russian SAM-site, the latter did not act.

The actual reasons for the lack of Russian reaction are as much related to the policy of the Putin government, as to the local terrain and the Russian military equipment. As described above, Moscow's military operation is run for Russian interests: despite its bravado on the international scene, Putin is not the least keen to provoke a war with the USA or other Western powers; at the same time, his interest is to maintain Bashar al-Assad in power in order to safeguard Russia's influence in the country – and this regardless of the continuous and growing Iranian encroachment on Syria. Correspondingly, although including SAMs with a theoretic range of 400 kilometres, air defences of the GRF have the sole purpose of protecting Russian military bases. All of these are located within the triangle between Hmeimim AB, the port of Tartus, and Masyaf (about 30 kilometres east of Tartus), where the Russians have also deployed the K-300P Bastion-P anti-ship and land-attack missile systems equipped with Oniks cruise missiles of the 11th Independent Coastal Missile Artillery Brigade.

Regardless of claimed or true capabilities of the Russian air defence systems in Syria, these remain rather limited. As of April 2017, they consisted of one battalion equipped with three S-400 SAM-sites, two SAM-sites equipped with Buk M1/M2 (ASCC-codes 'SA-11 Gadfly' and 'SA-17 Grizzly'), one SAM-site equipped with Tor M2 (ASCC-code 'SA-15 Gauntlet'), and four SAM-sites equipped with Pantsir-S1/S2 (ASCC-code 'SA-22 Greyhound'). Because of the an-Nusayriyah mountains, the radars of these units have only a very limited coverage of the airspace over northeastern Syria, and next to no coverage of southern and southeastern Syria. Indeed, because of the mountains, the VKS had no radar coverage over central Syria at all until an early warning radar station and a double S-300/400 SAM-site was constructed in the Masyaf area in May 2017. It was around the same time that the VKS started deploying its A-50 SRDLO aircraft at Hmeimim AB. The resulting complex of SAM and cruise-missile sites near Masyaf has included the only SyAAF unit directly integrated into the Russian IADS: the unit in question operates the antiquated P-14

A still from a video released by the Red Star Channel, showing the positions of at least two, probably three S-300/400 SAM-sites (each including four TELs, see colour section for details) protecting the cruise-missile battery near Masyaf as of early 2018. (Red Star/Russian Ministry of Defence)

With transnational jihadists of the HTS launching dozens of attacks with weaponised mini-UAVs on Hmeimim AB, the Russian air defences remained busy through the first half of 2018. This photograph shows a Pantsir-strike on an unknown UAV shot down over the main Russian base on 16 July 2018. (Syrian social media)

(ASCC-code 'Tall King') early warning radar: a 1950s-vintage system that is no longer in service with the Russian military, nor is Moscow's defence sector capable of providing support for it. Thus, it is maintained in operational condition with help from Belarus. The purpose of its integration into the Russian IADS is its long range, but also that it operates at wavelengths that are offering it at least a minimal ability to detect – even if not to effectively track – stealth aircraft.[188]

Geographically, the area covered by the Russian IADS is isolated from the areas covered by the IADS of the SyAAF: the central HQ of the SyAAF is still situated in an underground complex inside Mount Qasyoun, overlooking Damascus. From there, it is linked with help of electro-optical cables to one divisional HQ for air defences of Damascus, and another divisional HQ for air defences of Homs (both of which consist of one Senezh mobile command post). However, the rugged terrain between Homs and Tartus prevents the construction of an electro-optical cable there. Finally, the Russians are not only sensible in regards of the Assad government causing a possible clash with Israel, the USA and allies, or about sharing the intelligence they are collecting with the Assad government, but also concerned about potential vulnerability of their IADS: the software of the later tends to become unstable and requires rebooting whenever one of its elements is disabled – whether due to combat damage or for any other reason. Therefore, they are not keen to effect a full integration of their IADS with the SyAAF's IADS. Instead, they maintain a one-way protocol exchange with help of troposcatters, only: this helps feed some radar information from the SyAAF IADS into the Russian IADS, enhancing its coverage over northern and central Syria.[189]

Precisely because of this situation, and because of repeated US, British, French, but especially Israeli air strikes on diverse IRGC-QF and Hezbollah positions in Syria (as well as Assad government forces cooperating with these), several times since 2017, a number of Russian officials have expressed the possibility of deliveries of S-300P (ASCC-code 'SA-20 Gargoyle') SAMs to Damascus. Indeed, in an interview to the RT on 30 May 2018, Bashar al-Assad confirmed that, 'Syria is seeking to improve its air defences'. However, as of the time this book went to press, the Kremlin continued delaying the related decision. The most obvious reason is that of financing: with the Syrian economy in tatters and a nearly worthless national budget, Damascus simply cannot afford to purchase any S-300s from Moscow – at least not without sponsoring from Iran, which – at least currently – is rather unlikely.[190]

CHAPTER 7
CONCLUSIONS

The Russian military intervention has effected a major turn-around in the Syrian War: it not only enabled the IRGC-QF to tilt the balance of forces in favour of the 'pro-Assad' camp, but – in combination with an unprecedented diplomatic and propaganda campaign that effected an isolation of the Syrian opposition on the domestic and the international level – proved crucial for an entire series of defeats of the insurgency and transnational jihadists. On the other hand, Syria became the testing ground for what is widely perceived as 're-established Russian military might': not only the MOD in Moscow, but also the Supreme Commander of the Russian Federation's military forces, President Putin, have boasting of combat testing of over 200 diverse new weapons systems in Syria.

According to official releases from Moscow, during the first two years of the campaign, the tactical aviation of the VKS and the Russian naval aviation has carried out more than 39,000 combat sorties, as listed in Tables 7 and 8, while suffering relatively few losses (Table 9). Through constant rotation of personnel deployed to Syria, the VKS has reportedly exposed up to 80 percent of its tactical aviation crews, and up to 95 percent of its army aviation troops to combat, too.[191] Certain is also that the Russian military has demonstrated the capability to learn and adapt to the lessons of this conflict. However, equipment and combat experience aside, the VKS has actually shown very little that is new: the majority – nearly 50 percent – of combat sorties were flown by its old Su-24Ms. That type was replaced by larger numbers of more-modern Su-30SMs and Su-34s only in late 2017. Moreover, an estimated 97 percent of air strikes have resulted in the release of unguided munitions from aircraft flying at relatively slow speeds while underway at medium altitudes – under conditions entirely unlikely to occur in the case of any kind of a major conventional conflict. Contrary to the war in Afghanistan for example, the majority of VKS operations essentially resemble 'training flights including the release of live ammunition'.

Although not mentioned by officials in Moscow for months, the VKS continued flying up to 30 air strikes against different targets in Syria every single day through 2018. This Su-34 was involved in bombing the last Daesh-controlled pocket in the Yarmour Basin, in the south-west of the country in July of the same year. (Russian Ministry of Defence)

Table 7: Known Number of VKS Aircraft Deployed in Syria, September 2015 – June 2018

30 Sep 2015	27 Feb 2016	20 Mar 2016	19 Jan 2017	21 Jun 2017	19 Aug 2017	10 May 2018
4 Su-34	8 Su-34	4 Su-35	4 Su-35	6 Su-35S	6 Su-27SM/35S	4 Su-35S
4 Su-30SM	4 Su-35	4 Su-34	4 Su-34	6 Su-34	6 Su-34	6 Su-34
12 Su-25SM	4 Su-30SM	4 Su-30SM	4 Su-30SM	4 Su-30SM	4 Su-30SM	12 Su-30SM
2 Su-25UB	12 Su-25		4 Su-25	4 Su-25	6 Su-25	6 Su-25
12 Su-24M	16 Su-24M	12 Su-24M	12 Su-24M	6 Su-24M	8 Su-24M	12 Su-24M
1 Il-20M	1 Il-20M	1 Il-20M		1 Il-20M	1 Il-20M	3 Il-20M
	1 Tu-214R			1 A-50U	1 A-50	2 A-50/50U
	1 An-30					

Table 8: Total Number of Sorties Reported as Flown by the VKS and Naval Aviation, 2015-2017[192]

Date	Sorties	Targets claimed as 'destroyed'
by 29 Oct 2015	1,391	1,623
by 24 Dec 2015	5,240	not available
by 22 Feb 2016	11,700	22,000
by 22 Dec 2016	18,800	71,000
by 26 Apr 2017	23,000	77,000
by 22 Dec 2017	34,000	not available
by 15 Aug 2018	39,000	121,466

Table 9: Losses of Russian Aircraft and Helicopters in Syria, 2015-2018[193]

Date	Aircraft Type	Location	Notes
1 Oct 2015	Su-25SM	northern Hama	hit by MANPAD, damaged
9 Oct 2015	Mi-24P	northern Hama	forced landing due to combat damage
24 Nov 2015	Su-24M	northern Lattakia	shot down by THK F-16C; pilot killed, navigator recovered
24 Nov 2015	Mi-8AMTSh	northern Lattakia	damaged by ground fire, then destroyed by BGM-71 on the ground; 1 killed
12 Apr 2016	Mi-28N	eastern Homs	flew into the ground, killing the crew of 2
14 May 2016	Mi-24/35 or Ka-52	T.4 AB	conflagration on air base, presumably leading to destruction of four helicopters; claimed as destroyed by Daesh
8 July 2016	Mi-35M	Palmyra	shot down by Daesh, 2 of crew recovered
1 Aug 2016	Mi-8AMTSh	eastern Idlib	shot down by ground fire, 5 of crew and passengers killed
3 Nov 2016	Mi-35M	Palmyra	made emergency landing; crew evacuated, the helicopter then destroyed by Daesh
13 Nov 2016	MiG-29KUB	Mediterranean Sea	crashed after arrestor cable snapped; pilot recovered from the sea
3 Dec 2016	Su-33	Mediterranean Sea	crashed after arrestor cable snapped; pilot recovered from the sea
6 Oct 2017	Mi-28N	Hama	forced landing, possibly due to combat damage
10 Oct 2017	Su-24M	Hmeimim AB	crashed on take-off, crew killed
31 Dec 2017	Mi-35M	Hama	hit power lines and crashed, 2 of the crew of 3 killed
3 Feb 2018	Su-25SM	southern Idlib	shot down by ground fire, pilot killed himself on the ground
6 Mar 2018	An-26	Hmeimim AB	crashed, killing 6 of the crew and 33 passengers
3 May 2018	Su-30SM	Hmeimim AB	crashed into the sea, crew of 2 killed
7 May 2018	Ka-52	Euphrates	shot down by Daesh, crew of 2 killed

This is not to say that the VKS learned nothing at all from this campaign. On the contrary: it drew highly valuable experiences in regards of organizing and running expeditionary operations, and in regards of introducing network-centric warfare to its methods of operations. However, the primary effect of the Russian application of air power in Syria was that of making the Syrian armed opposition more dependent on aid from abroad than ever before, and destroying or rendering dysfunctional the civic authorities in insurgent and jihadist-controlled parts of the country. Although the precision of their air strikes early on was certainly nothing worth boasting about, when combined with the decision of major Western powers to look the other way while VKS and SyAAF's bombs have converted millions of Syrians into homeless refugees abroad, and the military intervention has enabled Moscow to isolate the insurgency on the diplomatic level. Not only the USA, Great Britain, and France, but even Qatar and Kuwait, followed by Saudi Arabia, United Arab Emirates, and Jordan, have curbed provision of financing and other form of aid to exactly zero. The sole remaining foreign supporter, Turkey, found itself isolated on the international level, too – even from its allies within NATO. Moreover, whether because of the JCPOA or for other reasons, and irrespective of obvious threats for the security of Israel, the West has proved amazingly ignorant of the massive Iranian military intervention and the deployment of dozens of thousands of IRGC-QC-controlled Shi'a jihadists and other para-militaries from around the world, which in turn proved crucial for developments on the ground. This combination of factors – and not the Russian military or any kind of shiny modern arms – was the crucial reason for the Syrian insurgents failing to defend any of the areas they used to control in 2016 and 2017, and being brought to the verge of a complete defeat during the first half of 2018.

Something similar can be concluded about the Russian involvement in the war against the JAN/JFS/HTS and Daesh. For years before Moscow launched its intervention in Syria, its security services were fuelling the growth of extremist Islamist movements in the Middle East by forcing dozens of thousands of Russian Islamists – true or perceived – to go to Iraq and Syria. The majority of them have joined the IS, relatively few the JAN/JFS/HTS. While this might sound absurd, it is a well-substantiated matter of fact based on quite straightforward logic: 'better the "terrorists" to go abroad and fight in Syria, than to make troubles in Russia'.[194] In comparison, and with the exception of two offensives on Palmyra and one on Dayr az-Zawr, the Russian military's efforts against Daesh were often bordering on a farce: when not, their sole effective component was limited to the deployment of attack helicopters, a few Su-25s, and the FACs. Nevertheless, because of the IRGC-QF's tenacity in regards of pursuing the IS through eastern Syria, Moscow is in a position to declare itself 'victorious' in this regard too.

From that standpoint, the conclusion is on hand that the Russian military actually needs not be particularly effective in the ways it fights wars, and needs not make extensive use of the latest technology, including thousands of PGMs; indeed, in theory, it could be abysmally ineffective, and learn next to nothing from its experiences at all. However, as long as it is supported by sound manoeuvring on the international diplomatic scene, and a highly-effective propaganda campaign, it is creating the impression of being far more effective than the militaries and intelligence services of all the Western powers involved in the 17-years-old 'War on Terror' – combined. It is 'winning wars'. This is probably the major lesson of this conflict, at least for the top political and military leaders in Moscow, and for those officers that commanded the Russian forces in Syria (listed in Tables 9 and 10), but for foreign observers, too.

Precisely this is the actual tragedy of the Middle East – and Syria in particular. Ultimately, Moscow's game of poker in Syria is as doomed to fail as dozens of Western interventions in this part of the World over the last 100 years: because it failed to remove any of the principal reasons for the crisis, and brought no prospects of a better future for the majority of the local population, it also brought no promise of lasting peace.

Table 10: Known Commanders of GRF in Syrian Arab Republic, 2015-2018

Commander	Dates
Col-Gen Aleksander Dvornikov	August 2015 – July 2016
Lt-Gen Aleksander Zhuravlev	July 2016 – December 2016
Col-Gen Andrei Kartapolov	December 2016 – April 2017
Col-Gen Sergey Surovikin	April 2017 – December 2017
Col-Gen Aleksander Zhuravlev	December 2017 –

Table 11: Known Commanders of GRF Training Mission to Syrian Arab Army, 2015-2018

Commander	Dates
Maj-Gen Sergey Sevryukov	August 2015 – August 2016
Maj-Gen Peter Milyuhin	August 2016 – February 2017
Lt-Gen Valery Asapov	February 2017 – August 2017

BIBLIOGRAPHY

A Reckless Disregard for Civilian Lives: Russian airstrikes in Syria to December 31st (Airwars.org, 14 March 2016).

Bar, S., *Bashar's Syria: The Regime and its Strategic Worldview* (Herzliya: Institute for Policy and Strategy, IDC Herzliya, 2006).

Breaking Aleppo, (Washington DC, The Atlantic Council of the United States, 2017).

Butowski, P., *Russia's Warplanes, Volume 1: Russian-made Military Aircraft and Helicopters Today*, (Houston: Harpia Publishing LLC, 2015; ISBN 978-0-9854554-5-3)

Cooper, T., *Syrian Conflagration: The Civil War, 2011-2013* (Solihull: Helion & Co., 2015; ISBN 978-1-9102294-10-9).

Cooper, T., *MiG-23 Flogger in the Middle East: Mikoyan I Gurevich MiG-23 in Service in Algeria, Egypt, Iraq, Libya and Syria, 1973-2018* (Warwick: Helion & Co., 2018, ISBN 978-1-912390-32-8).

Cooper, T., Nicolle, D., with Nordeen, L., and Salti, P., *Arab MiGs, Volume 3: The June 1967 War* (Houston: Harpia Publishing, 2012, ISBN 978-09825539-9-2).

Cooper, T., Nicolle, D., with Nordeen, L., Salti, P., and Smisek, M., *Arab MiGs, Volume 4: Attrition War, 1967-1973* (Houston: Harpia Publishing, 2013, ISBN 978-09854554-1-5).

Cooper, T., Nicolle, D., with Müller, H., Nordeen, L., and Smisek, M., *Arab MiGs, Volume 5: October 1973 War, Part 1* (Houston: Harpia Publishing, 2014, ISBN 978-0-9854554-4-6).

Cooper, T., Nicolle, D., with Grandolini, A., Nordeen, L., and Smisek, M., *Arab MiGs, Volume 6: October 1973 War, Part 2* (Houston: Harpia Publishing, 2015, ISBN 978-0-9854554-6-0).

Gorenburg, D., *What Russia's Military Operation in Syria Can Tell Us About Advances in its Capabilities*, (PONARS Eurasia, Policy Memo No 424, March 2016).

Grau, Dr. L. W. & Bartles, C. K., *The Russian Way of War: Force Structure, Tactics, and Modernization of the Russian Ground Forces* (Fort Leavenworth: Foreign Military Studies Office, 2016).

Hoffman, D. E., *The Billion Dollar Spy: A True Story of Cold War Espionage and Betrayal* (New York: Anchor, 2016, ISBN 978-0345805973).

Institute for the Study of War (ISW), *Syria Project* (various online releases at *understandingwar.org*, 2012-2017).

Kainikara, Dr. S., *Red Air: Politics in Russian Air Power* (Boca Raton: Universal Publishers, ISBN: 978-1-58112-983-0).

Kheder Khaddour, *Strength in Weakness: The Syrian Army's Accidental Resilience* (Carnegie: Middle East Center, 14 March 2016).

Lambeth, B., *Russia's Air Power at the Crossroads*, (Santa Monica: RAND, 1996; IBSN: 0-8330-2426-4).

Lavrov, A., *The Russian Air Campaign in Syria: A Preliminary Analysis* (Moscow: Centre for Analysis of Strategies and Technologies, 2018).

Markovskiy, V., *Hot Skies over Afghanistan* (Tehnika Molodoschy, 2000).

Medical Facilities under Fire, Syrian Archive, April 2017

Shaw, I., with Santana, S., *Beyond the Horizon: The History of AEW&C Aircraft* (Houston: Harpia Publishing LLLC, 2014; ISBN: 978-0-9854554-3-9).

Yousaf, Brigadier M. & Adkin, M., *Afghanistan, the Bear Trap: The Defeat of a Superpower* (Havertown: Casemate, 1992, ISBN 0-9711709-2-4).

NOTES

1   For details on early protesting and defections, see *Syrian Conflagration* (details in Bibliography).

2   Probably the best related review was provided by Kyle Orton in the article 'What to do about Syria: Sectarianism and the Minorities', *kyleorton1991.wordpress.com*, on 24 December 2014.

3   Athanasios Dimadis & Robert Ford, 'What Went Wrong in Syria?', *FairObserver.com*, 21 December 2017.

4   For details on related developments in the 2011-2013 period, see *Syrian Conflagration* (details in Bibliography). As of early 2018, no reputable observer has provided clear evidence for countries like Turkey or Saudi Arabia ever funding the JAN, although there is no doubt that numerous of their citizens did join that group, while private persons from Kuwait, Qatar, and the United Arab Emirates have supported it by chance over time. Some of the Qatari funding also did reach Daesh.

5   For reasons of space, this narrative is concentrating on the Russian military intervention in Syria in period 2015-2018. Therefore, closer descriptions of US and allied operations against Daesh, their cooperation with the PKK/PYD and associated militias, of US-Turkish-NATO relations with regards to the same, and of the Turkish military interventions in Syria in 2016-2018 are left out.

6   '2004 Census', Syrian Central Bureau of Statistics, *cbssyr.org*; 'Provinces of Syria', *statoids.com*.

7   'Syrian Refugees: Biggest Humanitarian Crisis', *Middle East Star*, 28 August 2014; Daily chart, 'Syria's drained population', *The Economist*, 30 September 2015. Note that a survey amongst refugees in a UNHCR camp in Kilis, Turkey, in January 2014, has shown that 43 percent of these felt forced to run away because government forces had occupied the place where they live; 35 percent because the government forces threatened with violence if they would not leave, and 22 percent because the government destroyed their home (see, 'Why are Syrians leaving their Homes, Turkey Refugee Camp Survey', The Washington Post, 29 September 2015).

8   'How Iran Keeps Assad in Power in Syria', *Inside Iran*, 5 September 2011; 'Syria's Crisis: The long Road to Damascus; There are Signs that the Syrian Regime may become more violent', *The Economist*, 11 February 2012; Joby Warrick & Liz Sly, 'US Officials: Iran is stepping up lethal Aid to Syria', *Washington Post*, 2 March 2012; 'Iran investing big in Syria', *Iran Times*, 4 October 2013; 'The Interim Finance Minister: 15 Billion Dollars Iranian support to Assad', *syrianef.org*, 24. January 2014; Salam al-Saadi, 'Iran's Stakes in Syria's Economy', *Carnegie Endowment for International Peace*, 2 June 2015; 'Iran spends Billions to prop up Assad', *BloombergView.com*, 9 June 2015 & Ian Black, 'Iran's Shadowy influence in Syria's Maelstrom fuels Paranoia and Wariness', *The Guardian*, 22 September 2015.

9   Sam Dagher, 'Syrian Bomb Plot Marked Deadly Turn in Civil War', *The Wall Street Journal* (henceforth 'WSJ'), 19 December 2014; Josh Rogin, 'UN's Brahimi: Round One of Syria Peace Talks', *thedailybeast.com*; 'Insight – Syrian Government Guerrilla

Fighters being sent to Iran for Training', *Reuters*, 4 April 2013; Ian Black, 'Syrian regime document trove shows evidence of "industrial scale" killing of detainees', *The Guardian*, 21 January 2014.

10 For a detailed description of the dissolution of the Syrian armed forces in 2011 and 2012, see *Syrian Conflagration* (details in Bibliography). Further confirmation for the related conclusions was provided by interviews with diverse officers of the SyAAF (details in endnotes below), and – independently – by Lieutenant-Colonel Mikhail Khodarenok (V-PVO, ret.), in 'Here's why Assad's Army can't win the War in Syria' (in Russian), *Novaya Gazeta*, 6 September 2016.

11 Reportedly, differences between Bashar and Maher reached their high point in January 2017, when rumours surfaced about Bashar suffering a stroke and being hospitalized – but also about Maher and the IRGC-QF attempting to depose him. Accordingly, the coup was thwarted by Russian military forces, which quickly blocked Iranian agents in eleven different districts of Damascus and at Almazza Air Base. See, Bethan McKernan, 'Syrian President Bashar al-Assad reportedly suffering under "psychological pressure"', *The Independent*, 22 January 2017 & 'Pro-Opposition Syrian Journalist in Tweets and Posts: Russian Forces thwarted Maher al-Assad's Iran-backed Coup Attempt', *MEMRI*, 3 February 2017.

12 Conclusions based on about 30 years of research into the Iranian military, including dozens of interviews with native military officers.

13 'Bashar Assad: Iran's Red Line', *Radio Farda*, 15 September 2017 & 'Fate of Assad is Iran's red line: Velayati', *Tehran Times*, 7 December 2015.

14 M. Q. (active officer of the IRGC), interview provided on condition of anonymity, October 2013. Despite concerns about possible repercussions from Western powers, the IRGC-QF did – officially – confirm its presence in Syria as of summer 2012. For details, see Ali Alfoneh, 'What is Iran doing in Syria?', *Foreign Policy*, 21 September 2012.

15 For details on deployment of the 8th 'Najaf' Armoured Division in Syria, see *Syrian Conflagration*.

16 Dexter Filkins, 'The Shadow Commander', *The New Yorker*, 30 September 2013.

17 'Iran: Senior IRGC Official confirms Hamedani is Syrian Field Commander', *IranNewsUpdate.com*, 8 October 2014 & 'The Last Interview with Sardar Hamedania about Syria and 88 Intrigue' (in Farsi), *Otaghkhabar24.ir*, 22 October 2015.

18 M. Q., interview, October 2013. For additional details about this process, see *Syrian Conflagration*.

19 'The Last Interview with Sardar Hamedani about Syria and 88 Intrigue' (in Farsi), *Otaghkhabar24.ir*, 22 October 2015.

20 Salam al-Saadi, 'Iran's Stakes in Syria's Economy', *Carnegie Endowment for International Peace*, 2 June 2015; Bozorgmehr Sharafedin & Ellen Francis, 'Iran's Revolutionary Guards reaps economic rewards in Syria', *Reuters*, 19 January 2017.

21 Dr Majid Rafizadeh, 'Iran Buying Syria Lands, Territories, Properties', *Huffington Post*, 6 December 2017.

22 Christop Reuter, 'Why Assad Has Turned to Moscow for Help', *Der Spiegel*, 6 October 2015.

23 Bar, pp. 355-356.

24 Dexter Filkins, 'The Shadow Commander', *The New Yorker*, 30 September 2013 & Christop Reuter, 'Why Assad Has Turned to Moscow for Help', *Der Spiegel*, 6 October 2015. The most notable officials that fell victim to Assad's purges of those who opposed the growing Iranian influence were Generals Rustum Ghazaleh (Head of the Political Security Directorate), and Dhu al-Himma Shalish (former commander of the RGD). Ghazaleh was beaten to death and had his estate south of Damascus blown up in December 2014, while Shalih was accused of corruption and treason, and imprisoned in July 2015. Through their removal, the IRGC-QF obtained direct physical access to Bashar al-Assad.

25 'Iran repopulates Syria with Shia Muslims to help tighten regime's control', *The Guardian*; 14 January 2017; 'Assad officially joins foreign militias into Syrian Army in a Plan to Change Syrian Demography', *Qasioun News*, 14 June 2017; 'How a victorious Bashar al-Assad is changing Syria', *The Economist*, 28 June 2018.

26 Dexter Filkins, 'The Shadow Commander', *The New Yorker*, 30 September 2013 & 'World indebted to Resistance Axis for Beating Takfirism: General Soleimani', *Tasnim News Agency*, 18 January 2018.

27 Anne Barnard, Hwaida Saad and Eric Schmitt, 'An Eroding Syrian Army Points to Strain', *NYT*, 28 April 2015 & Christop Reuter, 'Why Assad Has Turned to Moscow for Help', *Der Spiegel*, 6 October 2015.

28 'How Iranian general plotted out Syrian assault in Moscow', *Reuters*, 6 October 2015.

29 'Iran Quds Chief Visited Russia despite UN Travel Ban: Iranian Official'; *Reuters*, 7 August 2015 & 'Syria's Assad praises Iran deal as a "great victory"', *AFP/Yahoo! News*, 14 July 2015.

30 For related documentation and conclusions, see the book-series *Arab MiGs* Volumes 3, 4, and 5 (details in Bibliography), and Cooper, *MiG-23 Flogger*, pp. 29-31.

31 Cooper, *MiG-23 Flogger*, pp. 29-31 & Mark N Katz, 'Putin's Foreign Policy Toward Syria', *MERIA*, March 2006.

32 John Stockhouse, 'Putin backs away from Assad regime', *The Globe and Mail*, 1 March 2012.

33 'Security Council fails to adopt draft resolution condemning Syria's crackdown on anti-government protestors, owing to veto by Russian Federation, China', *UN*, 4 October 2011; 'Security Council fails to adopt draft resolution on Syria as Russian Federation, China veto text supporting Arab League's proposed peace plan', *UN*, 4 February 2012; ; 'Security Council fails to adopt draft resolution on Syria that would have threatened sanctions, due to negative votes of China, Russian Federation', *UN*, 19 July 2012; 'Referral of Syria to International Criminal Court fails as negative votes prevent Security Council from adopting draft resolution', *UN*, 22 May 2014.

34 Nikolay Poroskov, 'Aleksandar Vladimirov: Russia and Syria are going to control the Mediterranean Sea and the Pipelines to Europe' (in Russian), *Gazeta Kultura*, 15 October 2016; Shaun Walker, 'Vladimir Putin accuses US of backing terrorism in Middle East', *The Guardian*, 22 October 2015; Viktor Baranec, 'Chief of General Staff Valery Gerasimov: "We defeated the forces of terrorism"' (in Russian), *Komosomolskaya Pravda*, 27 December 2017 & 'Insider Out: how Russia went wrong, as told from the inside', *The Economist*, 16 September 2017.

35 Manfred Hafner, Simone Tagliapietra and El Habib El Elandaloussi, 'Outlook for Oil and Gas in Southern and Eastern Mediterranean Countries,' *MEDPRO Technical Report* No. 18/ October 2012; Nikolay Poroskov, 'Aleksandar Vladimirov: Russia and Syria are going to control the Mediterranean Sea and the Pipelines to Europe' (in Russian), *Gazeta Kultura*, 15 October 2016 & Viktor Baranec, 'Chief of General Staff Valery Gerasimov: "We defeated the forces of terrorism"' (in Russian), *Komosomolskaya Pravda*, 27 December 2017.

36 'Lawmakers authorize use of Russian military force for anti-IS airstrikes in Syria', *TASS*, 30 September 2015.

37 Tania Ildefonso Ocampos, 'The legal basis for foreign military intervention in Syria', *MiddleEastEye.net*, 29 July 2016.

38 'Anti-Assad rallies rebuff Syrian presidential election plan', *Reuters*, 3 April 2014; 'Foreign Secretary responds to Syrian election result', 5 April 2014; 'US condemns Syrian presidential election as a "disgrace"', *Reuters*, 3 June 2014.

39 Bill Whitaker, 'The Road to Syria', *CBSNews.com*, 10 January 2016. Notably, Whitaker further observed, 'We got the sense Admiral Komoyedov is not crazy about the Syrian president, who has dropped bombs on his own people. The admiral used a derogatory term to describe Assad, then asked that we not repeat it on TV.' For similar commentary, see also Lieutenant-Colonel Mikhail Khodarenok (V-PVO, ret.), in 'Here's why Assad's Army can't win the War in Syria' (in Russian), *Novaya Gazeta*, 6 September 2016.

40 Tania Ildefonso Ocampos, 'The legal basis for foreign military intervention in Syria', *MiddleEastEye.net*, 29 July 2016.

41 Grau et all, p. 11.

42 Ibid, p. 59.

43 Russian Military Doctrine (in Russian), *kremlin.ru*, 5 February 2010 & Polina Sinovets & Bettina Renz, *Russia's 2014 Military Doctrine and beyond: threat perceptions, capabilities and ambitions* (Rome: NATO Defense College, July 2015).

44 Based on description of the situation in Syria provided by Lieutenant-Colonel Mikhail Khodarenok (V-PVO, ret.), in 'Here's why Assad's Army can't win the War in Syria' (in Russian), *Novaya Gazeta*, 6 September 2016. Note that Khodarenok's conclusions – including the figure of 120,000 'government troops' – were the same as cited by multiple Western sources as of 2015, for example by Jeremy Bender in, 'Here are all the problems with the reeling Syrian army', *Business Insider*, 1 May 2015. Other sources – for example Abdulrahman al-Masri in 'Analysis: The Fifth Corps and the State of the Syrian Army', *NewsDeeply*, 11 January 2017 – estimated the total manpower of the Assad governemnt in 2015 as '80,000-100,000'. Notably, when asked about their estimates for actual troop strenght of the Assad government as of 2015, SyAAF officers cited figures between 25,000 and 30,000 ('Assad', Su-24-pilot, SyAAF, interviews in February 2014, April 2015, May 2015, June 2015 etc.; 'Boudros', MiG-21-pilot, SyAAF, interviews in October 2008, November 2015 and February 2016; 'Duha', SyAADF-officer, interviews in March 2007, July 2013, November 2015, February 2016 and April 2018; 'Khalid', Su-22 pilot, interviews, December 2012, April 2013, November 2015, March 2016, May 2018; 'Mouhannad', MiG-21- and Su-22-pilot, SyAAF, interviews in June 2011, July 2013, December 2016 and April 2018; all names changed for reasons related to the personal safety of the source and their family).

45 Conclusions based on Grau et all, pp. 25-30 & 385; Lambeth, p. 262-264; Kainkara, pp. 285-287; Samuel Charap, 'Russia's Use of Military Force as a Foreign Policy Tool: is There a Logic?', *RAND*, October 2016.

46 For details, see Lambeth, *Russia's Air Power at the Crossroads*.

47 Stefan Büttner, 'Die neue russische Luftwaffe, 2010', *Fliegerrevue*, 7/2010; Stefan Büttner, 'New Look for the Russian Air Force', *Combat Aircraft*, 7/2010; Alexander Mladenov, 'Reforming a Formidable Foe', *AirForces Monthly*, 9/2010 & Alexander Mladenov, 'Back on the Beat', *AirForces Monthly*, 4/2012.

48 Alexander Mladenov, 'Reforming a Formidable Foe', *AirForces Monthly*, 9/2010 & Alexander Mladenov, 'Back on the Beat', *AirForces Monthly*, 4/2012.

49 Dr Eugene Kogan, 'Under the Cloak of the OAK', *Military Technology*, 4/2007 & Dr. Eugene Kogan, 'Restructuring the Russian Aerospace Industry', *Military Technology*, 8/2009.

50 Dr Gary K Busch, 'The Delusion of Russian Power', *ocnus.net*, 25 November 2016. For details on the Tolkachev Affair, see Hoffman, *The Billion Dollar Spy* (details in Bibliography).

51 Even some of the top Russian military commanders have publicly concluded that what the Russian defence sector is delivering to them is not only below Western, but also below the quality standards of the People's Republic of China – and much too expensive. For example, while commenting on the production of the T-14 main battle tank, Chief-of-Staff Ground Forces, Colonel-General Posnikov observed, 'It would be easier for us to buy three Leopards (German-made main battle tank) with this money', see Dr Gary K Busch, 'The Delusion of Russian Power', *ocnus.net*, 25 November 2016.

52 Unless stated otherwise, this and the following two sub-chapters are based on Butowski, *Modern Russian Warplanes*.

53 Ministry of Defence of the Russian Federation, 'Ros Tender: Supply of Product 170-1' (in Russian), *rostender.info*, 26 August 2015.

54 Alexander Mladenov, 'Reforming a Formidable Foe', *AirForcesMonthly*, September 2010.

55 Grau et all, p. 371.

56 Butowski, *Modern Russian Warplanes Volume 1*, pp. 168-171 & Shaw et all, *Beyond the Horizon*, pp .190-191.

57 'From Russia with Love: Syria's BTR-82As', *Oryx Blog (spioenkop. blogspot.com)*, 24 August 2015; 'Russia may be escalating Military Role in Syria', *Los Angeles Times* (henceforth LAT), 3 September 2015.

58 'First Report on How the Military built an Air Base in Syria from the Scratch', *Zvezda TV*, 10 June 2016

59 'Huge Russian military Planes land in Syria', *AFP/Yahoo!*, 9 September 2015 & 'Russian Troops join Combat in Syria – Sources', *Reuters*, 10 September 2015; 'Russia sending Advanced Air Defence Systems to Syria', *Reuters*, 12 September 2015; Eric Schmitt & Michael R Gordon, 'Russian Moves in Syria Widen Role in Mideast', *New York Times* (henceforth 'NYT'), 14 September 2015; 'Russian Military High Command warns that Moscow might build an Air Force Base in Syria', *Meduza.io*, 16 September 2015. Eventually, it turned out that the involved An-124s were used to deploy elements of a VKS' Pantsir–S1 SAM-site to Hmeimim AB.

60 'Russia sends Fighter Jets to Syria after talks with U.S.', *CNN*, 19 September 2015.

61 M. Q., interview, October 2015; 'Assad', interviews in August 2015 and March 2016.

62 Since August 2015, crews and aircraft were drawn from 47th (Independent) Mixed Aviation Regiment (Buturlinovka); 257th (Independent) Composite Aviation Regiment (Khabarovsk Kray); 277th Bomber Aviation Regiment (Komsomoslk-na-Amur), and 559th (Independent) Bomber Aviation Regiment (Morozovsk).

63 Since August 2015, crews and aircraft were drawn from 3rd Guards Fighter Aviation Regiment (Krymsk); 14th Fighter Aviation Regiment (Khalino); 22nd Fighter Aviation Regiment (Tsentralnaya Uglovaya); 23rd Fighter Aviation Regiment (Dzengi); 31st Guards Fighter Regiment (Millerovo); 120th Mixed Aviation Regiment (Domma), and 929th V. P. Chkalova State Test Flight Centre (Akhtubinsk).

64 Since August 2015, crews and aircraft were drawn from 18th Guards Assault Aviation Regiment (Chernigovka); 37th

Composite Aviation Regiment (Gvardeyskoye); 266th Assault Aviation Regiment (Step); 368th Assault Aviation Regiment (Budyonnovsk); 960th Assault Aviation Regiment (Primosko-Akhtarsk), and 999th Assault Aviation Regiment (Kant).

65 Since August 2015, crews and aircraft were drawn from the 4th Centre for Combat Application and Crew Training (Lipetsk); 11th Composite Aviation Regiment (Mrinovsk); 37th Composite Regiment (Gvardeyskoye); 98th (Independent) Mixed Aviation Regiment (Monchegorsk); 277th Bomber Aviation Regiment (Komsomolsk-on-Amur); 455th Bomber Aviation Regiment (Voronezh); 559th Bomber Aviation Regiment (Morozovsk), and 6980th Composite Aviation Regiment (former 2nd Composite Aviation Regiment; Chelyabisnk/Shagol).

66 Crews and aircraft drawn from 535th Independent Composite Transport Aviation Regiment (Rostov-na-Donu).

67 'Kremlin: Syria air strikes target "a list" of groups', al-Jazeera, 1 October 2015.

68 M. Q., interview, October 2015.

69 Aleksey Nikolskiy, 'Russian Military left Syria' (in Russian), Vedomosti, 25 June 2013. While the status of the Russian depot in Tartus was frequently overblown, that of three signals-intelligence-gathering facilities (like Center-S, jointly run by the Russian Osnaz GRU and one of the Syrian intelligence agenices at al-Harra, in the Dera'a governnorate, and overrun by the insurgents on 5 October 2014) remained entirely unknown and are rarely mentioned in the public (see 'Captured Russian spy facility reveals the extent of Russian aid to the Assad regime', Spioenkop, 6 October 2014).

70 'The Agreement on Deployment of RF Air Force Group is concluded for a limitless Period', RIA Novosti, 14 January 2016.

71 'Russian "Visitors" receive warm welcome in coastal Syria', Daily Star, 25 September 2015.

72 Data based on monitoring the activities of VKS transports with help of FlightRadar24.com, over a period of three months in 2015 by Thomas M, as posted on ACIG.info forum.

73 Ever since, replaced by contingents from the 61st and then the 336th Naval Infantry Brigades of similar size.

74 Personnel and aircraft drawn from the GRU and 368th Assault Aviation Regiment.

75 Since April 2018, the VKS has a minimum of a battery of 9K332 Tor M2 (ASCC/NATO-code 'SA-15 Gauntlet') SAMs deployed at Hmeimim AB, too.

76 Michael Kofman, 'Russia's Intervention in Syria: Lessons Learned', Center for Strategic & International Studies (CSIS), Panel, 13 January 2017.

77 'The Night Air Strikes on Militant Objects' (in Russian), MOD YouTube channel, 1 October 2015 & 'Russia involved 10 reconnaissance Satellites in Syria Operation', TASS, 17 November 2015.

78 'Assad', interview, March 2016; 'Boudros', interview, November 2015; 'Ismael' (Su-22-pilot, SyAAF), interview in November 2015, 'Khalid', interview, November 2015 & 'Talal' (SyAAF-officer), interview, November 2015 (all names changed for reasons related to the personal safety of the source and their family). Some of interviewed Syrian officers have stated that the SyAAF's Su-22-units even had to fly photo-reconnaissance missions on behalf of the Russians.

79 Kheder Khaddour, 'The Assad Regime's Hold on the Syrian State', Carnegie Endowment for International Peace, 8 July 2015; Alexander Starritt, 'Syria's local councils, not Assad, are the answer to ISIS', The Guardian, 14 December 2015; 'Rebel Democracy in Action', isqatannizam.wordpress.com, 26 April 2016;

Omran for Strategic Studies, 'The Political Role of Local Councils in Syria', OmranDirasat.org, 1 July 2016; Daniel Moritz-Rabson, 'In wartime Syria, local councils and civil institutions fill a gap', PBS.org, 31 July 2016; Mark Boothroyd, 'Self-Organizatin in the Syrian Revolution', isqatannizam.wordpress.com, 17 August 2016; 'Local Councils in Besieged Areas', isqatannizam.wordpress.com, 25 October 2016; Robin Yassin-Kassab & Leila al-Shami, 'Burning Country: Syrians in Revolution and War' (Pluto Press, 2016).

80 Aleksander Kolotylo, 'The Russian Su-35 in Syria', Red Star, 23 November 2016. For details on SyAAF air strikes on bakeries, food storage sites, water treatment facilities, but also major insurgent HQs, see Syrian Conflagration. For their explanation from the standpoint of military theory, see David H Ucko, 'The People are Revolting: An Anatomy of Authoritarian Counterinsurgency', Journal of Strategic Studies, 27 November 2015; Michael Kofman, 'A Comparative Guide to Russia's use of Force: Measure twice, invade once', WarOnTheRocks.com, 16 February 2017 & Mark Galeotti, 'I'm sorry for Creating the "Gerasimov Doctrine"', Foreign Policy, 5 March 2018. Note that CENTCOM was applying similar practices on certain occasions: for example, during the battle for Raqqa, in 2017, it first 'requested' all the civilians to leave, then declared the entire city as a target assuming the civilians have left.

81 For details, see MiG-23 in the Middle East and 'Soviet Tactical Trends since the October 1973 War', DIA, April 1977, CIA/FOIA/ERR.

82 For details on deployment of Krasuha-4 ESM system, see Mary-Ann Russon, 'Russia using electronic warfare to cloak its actions in Syria from ISIS and NATO', International Business Times (henceforth 'IBT'), 11 October 2015. Syrian sources with knowledge about the Russian ATMS and IADS deployed at Hmeimim AB stress that despite this 'tight' integration, individual SAM-sites are still usually operated on their own. According to them, the software used for integration is sensitive to any major change in the composition of the system: whenever some major element is added or deleted, the software needs a reboot. Correspondingly, the Russians should be concerned that, especially in the case of the destruction of one major element of their IADS, the entire system is likely to become unstable, perhaps even collapse. It is for similar reasons that the Russians never opted to integrate their ATMS/IADS with that of operated by the SyAAF.

83 Grau et all, p. 385.

84 Aleksandar Kolotylo, 'They Arm our Su-24M in Syria', Red Star, 26 October 2016.

85 MOD, Twitter release, 1 October 2015 & 'The Night Air Strikes on Militant Objects' (in Russian), MOD YouTube channel, 1 October 2015.

86 'Kremlin: Syria air strikes target "a list" of groups', al-Jazeera, 1 October 2015.

87 'Destruction of IS Arms Depot in Ma'arat an-Nauman', MOD YouTube channel, 2 October 2015 & 'Head of the GenStab of the Russian Armed Forces, Andrey Kartapolov's statement on the Activities of the RF Aviation Group in Syria', MOD YouTube channel, 3 October 2015.

88 'Assad', interview, March 2016; 'Boudros', interview, November 2015; 'Ismael', interview, November 2015, 'Khalid', interview, November 2015 & 'Talal', interview, November 2015.

89 https://www.youtube.com/watch?t=62&v=ndpq0VhQqHs & Basma Atassi, 'Russia accused of striking Civilian Targets in Syria', al-Jazeera, 2 October 2015.

90 Ironically, the GenStab in Moscow originally refused to buy any KAB-500S because of their high price. Indeed, it remains unclear if the weapon was ever officially acquired by the VKS and is currently in operational service: rather than this, it seems that either only a small stock was purchased, or only a few pre-production rounds 'combat tested' in Syria. For details, see 'Patent for self-guided stablized bomb' (in Russian), *ak_12 blog*, 10 October 2015. According to V. Markovkiy & I Pirhodchenko, in *Fighter-Bomber MiG-27* (a book published in Russian, by Exprit, 2005), when Ukraine was released into independence, in 1991, its air force inherited only 69 Kh-59 and 132 Kh-59M (ASCC-code 'AS-13 Kingbolt') missiles, and 1,769 missiles from the Kh-25 family (ASCC-code 'AS-10 Karen'). In comparison, over 35,000 of Hughes AGM-65 Maverick guided missiles were manufactured in the USA and several allied countries over the last 40 years. Furthermore, during the I Chechen War, only three percent of ordnance deployed by the Russian air force was guided. During the Soviet times, and for most of the last 30 years, only '1st class' pilots were allowed to fly aircraft equipped with PGMs because of the complexity of required weapons systems, and an average fighter-bomber regiment was allocated only five guided weapons a year for training purposes. Finally, PGMs were always considered 'first strike weapons': systems used mostly on first waves of an operation. Nevertheless, and rather absurdly, although repeatedly caught lying – only 1 in the first 15 videos claimed as showing 'high precision strikes on IGIL' was showing any kind of deployment of PGMs, and not one was related to attacks on Daesh – the MOD in Moscow continued bragging in similar style well into November and December 2015.

91 'New System "Gefest" Allows the use of Non-Korrected Ammunition as High Precision Weapons', *TASS*, 25 August 2017. This 'official line' is maintained until today.

92 'Su-24MK2', *Rosoboronexport* (advertising brochure), 2006.

93 CCIP stands for 'constantly computed impact point'. Its essence is the calculation provided by the weapons sighting element of the nav/attack system, which is constantly predicting the point of impact on the basis of the aircraft's speed and flight altitude, gravity, the selected weapon's launch velocity, the weapon's drag, wind and diverse other factors. Usually displayed on the HUD, the CCIP moves depending on where the computer predicts the selected weapon will hit. As in the case of the SVP-24, the CCIP can usually be combined with an autorelease system.

94 Tomislav Mesaric, 'Su-25SM Prepares for the Fight', *AirForces Monthly*, 04/2017.

95 'Source: sent to Syria, the Su-34 prepared to conduct network-centric warfare', *TASS*, 8 October 2015.

96 Aleksandar Kolotylo, 'Our FAC in Syria', *Red Star*, 20 October 2016.

97 Tomislav Mesaric, interviews, October 2015 – August 2017; 'Russia's GLONASS Satellite System to be fully operational in 2010', *RIA Novosti*, 7 June 2008; Tim Springer and Rolf Dach, 'GPS, GLONAS, and More', *GPS-World*, June 2010; Brian Harvey, *The Rebirth of the Russian Space Program* (Springer, 2007); 'Third Soyuz launch in a week bolsters GLONASS System', *SpaceFlight Now*, 26 April 2013; 'The GLONASS System was out of Service for the Second time in a Month' (in Russian), *Novaya Gazeta*, 15 April 2014 & Tomislav Mesaric, 'Su-25SM Prepares for the Fight', *AirForces Monthly*, 04/2017.

98 Nizar al-Farra, News, *Sama TV*, 22 September 2015; 'Russia opposes "lawless" pro-Assad Militias: Report', *NowMedia*, 29 September 2015.

99 For detailed coverage of SyAAF combat operations in the period 2011-2014, see *Syrian Conflagration* & author's articles: 'The Syrian Air Battle', *CombatAircraft*, 07/2013, 'Desperate or in Full Swing', *CombatAircraft*, 07/2014, 'Air Power in Decline', *AirForces Monthly*, 06/2017. Cross-examination of all available reports has shown that SyAAF has carried out about 40,000 combat sorties between July 2012 and December 2014.

100 'Assad', interviews February 2014-May 2018; 'Boudros', interviews March 2007-April 2018, 'Duha', interviews July 2013-April 2018; 'Hashim' (SyAAF-officer), July 2013 & November 2016; 'Khalid', interviews, December 2012-May 2018; 'Nabil' (SyAAF-officer), interview, July 2013; 'Talal' (SyAAF-officer), interview, December 2012

101 'Assad', interview, February 2014, 'Mouhannad', interview, July 2013; 'Talal', interview, December 2012. Mouhannad stressed, that the communication channels of the Ba'ath Party are used to disseminate 'sensitive' orders (like those for intentional air strikes on civilians, or involving deployment of chemical weapons), and that all relevant officers of every squadron must confirm the receipt of such orders with their signature.

102 'Russian Warships Fired Cruise Missiles at Syria', *Lenta.ru* & 'Russian missiles "hit IS in Syria from Caspian"', *BBC*, 7 October 2015. According to details released by the MOD in Moscow, the majority of targets for cruise missiles launched on that day were in the Ma'arat an-Nauman area, while few others were directed against targets roughly between western Aleppo and Idlib.

103 Fayyad was cousin of Hafez al-Assad, and in command of one of 3rd Armoured Division's units during the onslaught on Hama, in 1982. His son married a daughter of Hafez al-Assad's brother Rifa'at.

104 'Obama Administration Ends Effort to Train Syrians to Combat ISIS', *NYT*, 11 October 2015.

105 Michael Weiss, 'Russia's Giving ISIS An Air Force', *DailyBeast.com*, 8 October 2015.

106 Speech by Hassan Nasrallah aired on al-Manar TV, on 17 October, citing the death of Hassan Hussain al-Haj (aka 'Abu Muhammad'), one of its top military commanders, killed a week earlier. In the course of the same speech, Nasrallah boasted that his group's presence in Syria is, 'larger than ever before – qualitatively, quantitatively, and in equipment, because we are in a critical and definitive battle…'.

107 'Russians Pounded the 26th Brigade NDF north of Homs', *NowMedia*, 16 October 2015 & 'Russia/Syria: Possibly Unlawful Russian Air Strikes: Entire Extended Family Killed in Homs', *HRW*, 25 October 2015.

108 'Talal', interview, December 2016.

109 Phillip Smyth, 'Iran's Losing Major Operatives in Syria', *TheDailyBeast.com*, 14 October 2015. Hamedani was acting commander IRGC-QF in Syria at the time of his death, which was probably related to his visit to either one of Iranian-controlled Iraqi Shi'a militias, or during the visit to the Liwa al-Qods al-Filistini – which was his favourite unit in Syria, and something like his 'main instrument' since October 2014, when its combatants saved him during an attack of the US-supported Harakat Hazzm (FSyA) on Hindarat.

110 Data based on monitoring of related activities with help of *FlightRadar24.com*, by Thomas M, as posted on *ACIG.info* forum. Additional details from 'Assad Allies, including Iranians, prepare ground attack in Syria: Sources', *Reuters*, 1 October 2016 & Sam Dagher, 'Iran Expands Role in Syria in Conjunction With Russia'a Airstrikes', *WSJ*, 2 October 2015.

111 'Two Turkish Jets harassed on Syrian Border', *Hurriyet*, 5 October 2015; 'Syria Conflict: Turkish jets "intercept Russian plane"', *BBC*, 5 October 2015; 'Russia says Violation of Turkish Airspace was 'Navigational Error''', *Hurriyet*, 5 October 2015 & 'Statement by the North Atlantic Council on incursions into Turkey's airspace by Russian Aircraft', NATO, 5 October 2015.

112 'Show me your ID: Russian Sukhoi Su-30 gets near US jet over Syria for Identification', *RT*, 14 October 2015; 'Russian military informs Turkish military about air space violations', *The Daily Star*, 15 October 2016; 'Obama Says Deal Reached with Russia to Avert Syria Air Conflicts', *Bloomberg*, 16 October 2015 & Orhan Coskun, 'Turkey shoots down drone near Syria, US suspects Russian origin', *Reuters*, 16 October 2015.

113 'Turkey: Syrians Pushed Back at the Border', *HRW*, 23 November 2015; 'Turkey caught between aiding Turkmen and economic dependence on Russia', *The Guardian*, 24 November 2015.

114 'Boudros', interview, November 2015; 'Duha', interview, November 2015; 'Ismael', interview, November 2015, 'Khalid', interview, November 2015, 'Mohammad' (MiG-21/23-pilot, SyAAF, name changed for reasons related to the personal safety of the source and their family), March 2016 & 'Third Russian air strike on Syrian rebel group kills leader', *Reuters*, 1 November 2015. Details about what exactly happened on 18 October 2015 at Jebel Nabi Younis remain unclear and hotly disputed. Social media from parts of Syria controlled by the Assad regime reported the death of Colonel Maher Zayoud on that date, and in that area; diverse other reports cited the death of up to 11 officers, including 'at least three Russians', while some Ukrainian activists reported the death of up to 26 Russians, 'possibly mercenaries'. Notably, even reporting by the Russian MOD about this period was completely confusing. On 20 October, this claimed the capture of Talbiseh, in the RTP, and 'supported' that claim by publishing corresponding maps, only to announce air strikes on Talbiseh, later during the same media briefing. Sufficient to say that Talbiseh was never 'captured': it was abandoned by insurgents following another of the 'cease-fire agreements', in May 2018.

115 'Russian Air Group in Syria has destroyed more than 1,600 Objects of Terrorists in Syria in a Month', *Interfax*, 30 October 2015.

116 'Harsh Conditions are foiling Russian Jets in Syria', *USA Today*, 25 October 2015; Irek Murtazin, 'Russia should not get stuck in the Middle East', *Novaya Gazeta*, 12 October 2015.

117 'Video of Russian Aviation Strike on the Base Camp of Militants in Rakka' (in Russian), *MOD YouTube channel*, 26 November 2015 & Butowski, *Russia's Warplanes*, pp. 33-34.

118 Data about the 'results' of diverse Russian cruise missile strikes from November 2015 is based on cross-examination of dozens of related reports in the Syrian social media.

119 'Syria Feature: Russia's Bombed "ISIS Oil Refinery" is a Vital Water Treatment Plant', *EA Worldview*, 4 December 2015. Even the cummulative effects of the Operation Tidal Wave II began to show only a month later, when Daesh was forced to decrease the wages of its combatants by half, see 'ISIS cuts fighter's salaries due to exceptional circumstances', *CNBC*, 20 January 2016.

120 Will Stewart, Sara Malm, Larisa Brown, 'Rescued Russian pilot vows pay back for his lost co-pilot after Turks shot him down with no warning', *Mail Online*, 25 November 2015.

121 'Video of the S-400 Surface-to-Air Missile System in Syria', *Zvezda TV*, 26 November 2015. Notably, upon watching the same video, multiple sources with first-hand-experience on the latest Russian SAM-systems have described the system in question as 'S-350': a system including radar components of the S-400, but still largely consisting of elements from the S-300.

122 'Four Syrian Hospitals bombed since Russian airstrikes began, Doctors say', *The Guardian*, 22 October 2015. Out of about 60 videos released by the MOD in Moscow by 24 October 2015, 48 were geolocated by the crowdfunded project *Bellingcat.com* (see articles like 'What Russia's Own Videos and Maps Reveal About Who They Are Bombing in Syria', from 26 October 2015, or 'Dataset of Russian attacks Against Syria's Civilians', from 13 May 2016): of these, only one (in digits: 1) was confirmed as actually showing an attack on any kind of targets in the Daesh-controlled parts of Syria. The majority of the rest was clearly indicative of intentional attacks on civilian facilities in insurgent-controlled areas. For a typical example of the CBU-controversy, see 'Ministry of Defence: Russia does not use Cluster Bombs in Syria', *RT*, 23 December 2015.

123 'Guardians of the Sky of the Motherland', *Red Star*, 19 February 2016 & Airwars, *Reckless Disregard* (for details see Bibliography).

124 A. R. & B. N. (officers of armed Syrian opposition; names withheld for reasons related to the personal safety of the source and their family), interviews, November 2015 & March 2016. According to the same sources, by the time the fighting in this part in Syria died away, in March 2016, the 1st Coastal Division was down from 2,800 to about 800-900 combatants.

125 De-facto cut off from the outside world, and known for maintaining friendly relations to the Assad government at least since the late 1980s, the PKK/PYD/YPG/YPJ-conglomerate in control of the Afrin enclave was never a part of the SDF, and thus never supported by the USA.

126 'Syria Civil War: President Assad's Forces cut off last Rebel Supply Line to Aleppo raising Fears of huge Humanitarian Crisis', *Independent*, 3 February 2016 & 'Kurds poised to capture Syrian rebel-held airbase', 11 February 2016.

127 'Assad', interview, March 2016.

128 There is circumstantial evidence that, amid high tensions caused by intensive Russian bombardment of targets very close to the Turkish border, and the fact that several shells fired either by the Russian or the forces of the Assad government that fell north of the border, another aerial clash between the THK, the SyAAF and the VKS might have occurred on 26 February 2016. The same is likely to have included at least a few of about 20 F-16s known to have been airborne at that time, and one or more Su-24MK2s of the SyAAF. More precise details remain elusive, but following reports in the Turkish social media about the appearance of three F-16, then a 'big detonation', and then the finding of the wreckage of an AIM-120C – all of this in the Kislak area, in the Hatay province of Turkey – rumours began to spread about either an 'unknown UAV', or a Su-24 being shot down. Immediately afterwards, all the related reporting suddenly ceased, and only one related media-report was released in the public: 'Search begins for reported unmanned aerial vehicle near Syrian border', *Dogan News Agency*, 26 Februar 2016.

129 Numbers based on contemporary satellite photographs published by diverse online sources (for example, see Samir/@obretix on Twitter).

130 'Russian air strikes near Palmyra as Syrian troops advance', *Mail Online*, 15 March 2016; 'Syrian army aims for eastward advance with Palmyra attack', *The Daily Star*, 16 March 2016; '26 die as Russian jets back Syrian advance near Palmyra', *Reuters*, 16 March 2016; 'ISIS kills five Russian soldiers during fighting in Syria', *Mail Online*, 22 March 2016; 'Russian officer killed near Palmyra in Syria', *Mail Online*, 24 March 2016; Dominic

Evans, 'Syrian Army, with Russian air support, advances inside Palmyra', *Reuters*, 27 March 2016.

131 'Discerning Damage to a Crucial Syrian Air Base', *STRATFOR*, 24 May 2016. Ironically, nearly all of the world-wide MSN subsequently forwarded Daesh's claim that it destroyed four Russian helicopters in an artillery attack. Note that the exact type of helicopters destroyed on this occasion remains unknown. Because satellite photographs from 14 May 2016 have shown four intact Mi-24/35s parked at the part of T.4 AB gutted by the subsequent conflagration, most of sources have reported the destruction of Mi-24/35s. However, there are reports that the helicopters in question were actually Ka-52s. Note that not one of four helicopters of this type known as deployed to Syria a month earlier was ever sighted airborne over the country again.

132 'Syria's Ambassador to Russia urges all countries to join Syria and Russia against terrorism', *SANA*, 1 October 2015.

133 'Iran commits Hamadan airbase to Russia for as long as needed', *RT*, 21 August 2016; 'Iran – Constitution' (unofficial translation from Farsi to English, adapted to ICL standards), *University of Bern*, 29 May 2010 & Dr Eugene Kogan, 'Russian-Iranian Relations: A Mixed Bag', *European Security & Defence*, December 2017.

134 Aleppo, with a population of 2.132 million according to the 2004 census, was split into two by an insurgent advance into the eastern and southern parts of the city, in July 2012. The following years of fighting depleted the population, but nobody had a clear idea to what degree. By early 2016, the UN has estimated the population of eastern Aleppo to be about 300,000 ('UNICEF Flash Update Syria Crisis', *UNICEF*, 13 February 2016), and then to about 138,000 by August of the same year ('Monitoring of the Protection Situaiton in Besieged East Aleppo City', *Syria Protection Cluster (Turkey)*, November 2016.

135 According to reports like 'Who's involved in the Rebels' Aleppo Offensive?', *The New Arab*, 28 October 2018 or Tom Miles, 'Aleppo's Jabhat Fateh al-Sham Fighters Far Fewer than UN Says', *Reuters*, 14 October 2016, around 8,000 Syrian insurgents – including about 100-200 affiliated with the JFS – were left inside eastern Aleppo by the time.

136 *Breaking Aleppo*, pp. 9-10, 14.

137 'Boris Johnson: strong evidence Russia carried out strike on UN convoy in Syria', *The Guardian*, 21 September 2016; 'Syrian Jets Unable to Fly by Night; Not Behind Attack on Aid Convoy Near Aleppo', *Sputnik*, 21 September 2016; 'Lavrov rejects claims that aid convoy was hit by Syrian Air Force', *TASS*, 21 September 2016.

138 Tom Perry, Suleiman al-Khalidi, 'Heavy air strikes hit rebel road to Syria's Aleppo', *Reuters*, 22 May 2016 ; 'Crazy bloody night in Aleppo: more than 50 raids and barrel bombs, 33 civilians killed and 31 trucks of WFP convoy targeted', *Aleppo24*, 19 September 2016; 'Aleppo aerial campaign deliberately targeted hospitals and humanitarian convoy amounting to war crimes, while armed groups' indiscriminate shelling terrorised civilians – UN Commission', *UN*, 1 March 2017; 'UN Investigators Say Syria Bombed Convoy and Did So Deliberately', *NYT*, 2 March 2017; 'From Paradise to Hell: How an Aid Convoy in Syria Was Blown Apart', *NYT*, 17 October 2016.

139 'Assad or We Burn the Country', *The Atlantic Council of the United States*, April 2017 & 'Aleppo aerial campaign deliberately targeted hospitals and humanitarian convoy amounting to war crimes, while armed groups' indiscriminate shelling terrorised civilians – UN Commission', *UN*, 1 March 2017.

140 'WHO condems massive attacks on five hosptials in Syria', *WHO*, 16 November 2016; ,Syria: Fatal airstrike on maternity hospital a potential war crime', *Amnesty International*, 29 July 2016; 'Hospitals hit repeatedly by Russian and Syrian airstrikes, condemning hundreds of wounded to certain death', *MSF*, 5 October 2016; 'Aleppo hospital bombed again as Assad vows to clean the city', *The Guardian*, 14 October 2016; 'Eastern Aleppo hospitals damaged in 23 attacks since July', *MSF*, 7 July 2016; 'Last Hosptial in Aleppo', *DFR Lab*, 16 January 2017.

141 'Russian Defense Minister General of the Army Sergei Shoigu announced the cease of air strikes in the Aleppo region', *MOD*, 18 October 2016. By then independent researchers had recorded a total of 13 attacks using CBUs filled with incendiary ammunition on eastern Aleppo, includng against the al-Mashhad neighbourhood (centre of Aleppo, on 7 August), in District 1070 (2 September), in Bustan al-Qasr (22 September), in al-Bab (23 September), as-Salhin (24 September), Mashhad, Fardous and Bab an-Nayrab (25 September), Sha'ar (30 September 2016), and on Myassar district (14 October), see *Breaking Aleppo*, pp. 34-35 & 'Aleppo aerial campaign deliberately targeted hospitals and humanitarian convoy amounting to war crimes, while armed groups' indiscriminate shelling terrorised civilians – UN Commission', *UN*, 1 March 2017.

142 *Breaking Aleppo*, p. 15. No less disgusting were attacks with chemical weapons – although there is no evidence that any of these saw any kind of Russian involvement. The majority of those that have hit eastern Aleppo – as on 2 and 10 August 2016, twice on 20 November, on 23 November, and multiple times during the following days – were flown by diverse SyAAF helicopters operated from a newly-constructed helidrome in as-Safira, and included the deployment of tanks filled with chlorine.

143 'Airstrikes on school in Hass: what we know', *CITeam.org,* 31 October 2016.

144 The use of the social media in Syria was always heavily restricted and strictly scrutinised by multiple security services of the Assad government. Although numerous individuals are pretending to act independently from the government, especially presences in English language – including several 'news agencies' supposedly based in Lebanon – are all either sanctioned by the government and its security services, or actually run by the same, or by Hezbollah/Lebanon.

145 *Breaking Aleppo*, p. 5. Largely unnoticed in the public that it was at the same time that another of the bizzare episodes in this war took place. On 15 November 2016, *The Tehran Times* published the article 'IRGC: US struck Iran-built Arms Factory in Syria'. In the article in question, Brigadier-General Amir Ali Hajizadeh (commander of the IRGC Air & Space Force) bitterly complained that the US 'has targeted and completely demolished' an arms factory built by Iran in Syria. Actually, the attack in question was undertaken by the insurgent group Jaysh al-Mujhidden, which plastered as-Safira with BM-21 artillery rockets.

146 *Breaking Aleppo*, p. 5.

147 'The Ministry of Defence announced 420 sorties of aviation from Admiral Kuznetsov in Syria' (in Russian), *RBC*, 6 January 2017 & 'Russia steps up military presence in Syria, despite Putin's promise', *FoxNews,* 11 January 2017.

148 'Russia announces ceasefire in Syria from midnight', *Reuters*, 29 December 2016; 'Syria: Russian aircraft unit prepares to depart Syria as scale-back continues', *RT*, 17 January 2017; Tomislav Mesaric, 'Su-25SM prepares for the Fight', *AirForces Monthly*, 04/2017.

149 'Russian Media Attacks Assad for Failure to Defend Damascus', *The Syrian Observer*, 24 March 2017.

150 Based on account of an anonymous combatant from the Tiger Force, widely circulated in pro-Assad, English-language social media, and cross-examination of reporting about VKS' air strikes. Ironically, at least 14 of the abandoned tanks captured by Daesh were subsequently claimed as destroyed by US forces, see 'Airstrikes destroy ISIL's captured tanks', *CENTCOM*, 16 December 2016.

151 Q. M., interview, May 2017; 'Assad', interview, June 2017; 'Boudros', interview, April 2018; 'Duha', interview, April 2018; 'Mouhannad', interview, May 2017; 'Talal', interview, June 2017.

152 Ibid & cross-examination of social media reports about air strikes flown by the VKS and SyAAF.

153 Based on cross-examination of reporting in the social media (especially by Sentry Syria), and interviews with 'Assad', 'Boudros', 'Duha', and 'Talal'.

154 Tomislav Mesaric, 'Su-25SM prepares for the Fight', *AirForces Monthly*, 04/2017.

155 Based on cross-examination of reporting in the social media, (especially by Sentry Syria, a service organized in insurgent-controlled areas with help of social media that provided timely warnings about every take-off from major air bases all around the country); interviews with 'Assad', 'Boudros', 'Duha', and 'Talal'; 'Medical Facilities under Fire', *Syrian Archive*, April 2017 & 'Russian Air Strikes in Syria, March 20 – April 25, 2017', *ISW*, 30 April 2017.

156 Data based on a table purportedly prepared by the MOD, and circulated in the Russian social media. According to the MOD ('S. Shoygu annual report', *MOD*, 22 December 2017), the VKS' air defences in Syria shot down 16 UAVs and 53 rockets in 2017 alone.

157 'Summary of Claims Surrounding the Khan Sheikhoun Chemical Attack', *Bellingcat.com*, 4 July 2017; 'Did Russia Accidentaly Provide the Best Evidence of the Syrian Government's Involvement in Sarin Attacks?', *Bellingcat.com*, 13 November 2017; cross-examination of reporting in the social media, by Sentry Syria, and interviews with 'Assad', 'Boudros', 'Duha', and 'Talal'.

158 'ISI first to analyze Shayrat airfield missile attack', *ImageSatIntl. com*, 15 May 2017. A cross-examination of videos and photographs taken after the US attack has turned out evidence for destruction of at least three MiG-23s and nine Su-22s, while four additional fighter-bombers were rendered inoperable.

159 Markovskiy, *Hot Skies over Afghanistan*, p. 33.

160 'Assad', interview, June 2017; 'Boudros', interview, April 2018; 'Duha', interview, March 2017; 'Talal', interview, December 2016.

161 Barbara Starr, Ryan Browne & Zachary Cohen, 'US Aircraft shoots down Iranian-made drone in Syria', *CNN*, 9 June 2017. The aircraft that scored the kill against the Shahed-129 was an F-15E of the USAF. Another IRGC-QF-operated Shahed-129 was shot down by USAF F-15Es on 20 June. Further to this, on 15 and 16 June 2017, SyAAF MiG-23MLDs reportedly shot down two Italian-made Selex ES Falco UAVs operated by Jordan – using R-24R missiles.

162 'Hussam', interview, April 2018; 'Khalid', interview, December 2017.

163 'Syrian forces break ISIS siege of Deir ez-Zor airfield after Russian air strike', *TASS*, 9 September 2017.

164 'VKS increased the number of sorties to 100 per day in the Deir-ez-Zor area', *Interfax*, 6 November 2017.

165 'Tu-22M3 bombers and submarine Kolpino hit ISIS infrastructure near Abu Kamal', *Russsian MOD*, 3 November 2017.

166 The MiG-29SMTs were drawn from the 116th Fighter Aviation Employment Centre in Astrakhan. They were present in Syria from September until December 2017.

167 Based on cross-examination of reporting in the social media, by Sentry Syria, and interviews with 'Assad', 'Boudros', 'Duha', and 'Talal', April 2018.

168 'Russia: Putin Makes Surprise Visit to Syria, Announces Start of Troop Withdrawal', *STRATFOR*, 11 December 2017; 'Putin declares complete victory on both banks of Euphrates in Syria', *Reuters*, 6 December 2017; 'Putin announces Russian troop withdrawal from Syria during visit', *BBC*, 7 December 2017; 'Syria: Russia Will Have Permanent Presence at Tartus, Hmeymim', *STRATFOR*, 27 December 2017.

169 'Briefing', *MOD*, 11 January 2018. According to reports published in the Syrian social media, dozens of such attacks were launched ever since – but most have been spoiled by Russian air defences. At least 15 UAV attacks on Hmeimim were registered in July 2018 alone.

170 'Syria: Government Forces Continue Offensive to Recapture Abu Zuhour Air Base', *STRATFOR*, 10 January 2018; 'Syria: Russian Warplane Shot Down over Idlib Province'; *STRATFOR*, 3 February 2018.

171 'Briefing', *MOD*, 5 February 2018.

172 Alternative reports have indicated an explosion of the ordnance carried by this Su-24MK2 as the reason for its loss.

173 'Duha', interview, July 2013; 'Hashim', interview, July 2013; 'Nabil' (SyAAF-officer, name changed for reasons related to the personal safety of the source and their family), interview, November 2016.

174 'ISIS retreating in Syria, missile system destroyed, 33 targets hit – Russian military', *RT*, 15 October 2015. Surprisingly enough, Moscow subsequently withdrew its announcement that it was one of VKS' air strikes that killed the powerful leader of the JAI, Zahran Alloush, on 25 December 2015. The attack in question was actually flown by two SyAAF Su-24MK2s.

175 'Alleged PHOTO, VIDEO of Russian Su-57 Fifth Gen Jet in Syria Released on Twitter', *Sputnik*, 22 February 2018; 'Possible Reason for Deployment of Russia's 5th Gen Su-57 to Syria Revealed', *Sputnik*, 26 February 2018; 'Putin's Newest Stealth Fighters are Nonoperational. So Why Deploy Them to Syria?', *Haaretz*, 26 February 2018; 'Su-57 fighter launch an advanced cruise missile in Syria', *MOD YouTube channel*, 25 May 2018

176 'The siege and recapture of eastern Ghouta', *UN, Human Rights Council*, (details in Bibliography) & 'Syria: Hundreds killed by Airstrikes Pounding Rebel Enclave Near Damascus', *STRATFOR*, 24 February, 2018.

177 Ibid.

178 Theodore Schleifer & Barbara Starr, 'Russia denies bombing US-supported rebels near Jordan border', *CNN*, 19 June 2016.

179 Eric Schmidt, 'In Syria's Skies, Close Calls with Russian Warplanes', *NYT*, 8 December 2017; Oriana Pawlyk, *Military. com*, 14 December 2017.

180 'Moscow denies Russian Jets intercepted by US F-22 in Syria', *Sputnik*, 14 December 2017.

181 'Duha', interview, April 2018, 'Talal', interview, April 2018.

182 Ibid & OIR (Operation Inherent Resolve) Spokesman, 'Unprovoked attack by Syrian pro-regime forces prompts Coalition defensive strikes', 7 February 2018; SDF Spokesman, 'US airforce has destroyed more than 20 SAA vehicles', 7

February 2018; 'Syria War: Assad's Government accuses US of Massacre', *BBC*, 8 February 2018; Christoph Reuter, 'The Truth about the Russian Deaths in Syria', *Der Spiegel*, 2 March 2018.

183 Christoph Reuter, 'The Truth about the Russian Deaths in Syria', *Der Spiegel*, 2 March 2018 & 'US says clash averted with Russian mercenaries in Syria', *AFP/Mail Online*, 27 March 2018. According to multiple Syrian sources interviewed independently, reports – mostly launched by Russian nationalists on the social media – according to which '100, 200, 300' or 'as many as 600' Russians had been killed in the fighting at Khusham and Tabya clash are wildly exaggerated.

184 The Saeqeh UAV is roughly based on the US-made RQ-170 Sentinel UAV, one of which is known to have been forced to land inside Iran in 2011.

185 Hagay Hacohen, 'Israeli F-16 Pilots speak: the Force of the Blast could have killed us', *Jerusalem Post*, 11 February 2018. This was the first Israeli fighter jet confirmed as shot down in combat since 16 November 1983, when an Israeli Aircraft Industries (IAI) Kfir was felled by Syrian-operated SA-8s over Bhamdoun, in Lebanon.

186 'Russia: Complete Iranian withdrawal from Syria is "absolutely unrealistic"', *The Times of Israel*, 1 August 2018.

187 Mikhail Hodarenok, 'S-400 did not Respond to Shayrat' (in Russian), *Gazeta.ru*, 7 April 2017; Konstantin Sivkov, 'The Purpose of Tomahawks is not Syria, but Moscow' (in Russian) & Nikolay Novichkov, 'Tomahawks – for Russian Army: a blow on Shayrat AB has become an invaluable Gift for our Air Defence', *Voyenno Promyshlennyy Kuryer*, 10 April 2017. While indisputable and clearly confirmed on numerous occasions, the presence of the Russian S-300 SAM-site in the area between Tartus and Masyaf remains the issue of some controversy. In October 2016, US sources reported the deployment of the S-300V4 (ASCC/ NATO-code 'SA-23 Gladiator') long-range SAM-system to Syria for the first time. The presence of a S-300 system was subsequently confirmed by Major-General Igor Konashenkov, MOD's spokesman. However, no related photographs or videos were ever released, and what Konashenkov has mentioned was the 'Fort' – or S-300P or a newer S-300PM system, not the S-300V4. Satellite photographs and videos released by the Russian MOD in late 2017 have shown the deployment of SAMs similar to the S-400 system protecting Hmeimim AB. Thus, it is possible – although unonfirmed – that the Russiam Army has deployed one or two batteries (perhaps a full battalion of three batteries) to Syria in a period of about eight months, between October 2016 and June 2017, but this remains unconfirmed. Instead, the second S-400 system was deployed in the same position sometime between April and July 2017.

188 'Duha', interview, April 2018, 'Talal', interview, April 2018.

189 Ibid.

190 For comparison purposes: while, as described in Chapter 2, the annual national budget of the Assad government declined to US$5.1 billion in 2017, it is known that Egypt paid more than US$1 billion for the S-300VM Antey-2500 variant of the S-300 system already in 2014. It is unlikely that the system became any cheaper in the meantime.

191 'More than 48 thousand Russian military received combat experience in Syria', *RIA Novosti*, 22 December 2017.

192 Lavrov, 'The Russian Air Campaign in Syria' (see Bibliography for details).

193 Table by Milos Sipos, based on reporting in the MSN and social media.

194 Elena Milashina, 'Russia is sending Jihadists to Join the ISIS', *Novaya Gazeta*, September 2015.